Early Childhood Education

ANNIE L. BUTLER
Indiana University

Early Childhood Education

Planning and Administering Programs

D. VAN NOSTRAND COMPANY
New York / Cincinnati / Toronto / London / Melbourne

Cover Illustration: Courtesy of Educational Facilities Laboratories, photographer Bob Perron

D. Van Nostrand Company Regional Offices:
New York Cincinnati Millbrae

D. Van Nostrand Company International Offices:
London Toronto Melbourne

Library of Congress Catalog Card Number 74-7570
ISBN: 0-442-20897-9

Published by D. Van Nostrand Company
450 West 33rd Street, New York, N.Y. 10001

Published simultaneously in Canada by
Van Nostrand Reinhold Ltd.

10 9 8 7 6 5 4

Preface

THIS BOOK IS INTENDED FOR THOSE WHO ADMINISTER EARLY childhood programs and for students and in-service teachers interested in the planning and administration of early childhood programs. It differs from most books on early childhood education in that it does not deal primarily with the specific curriculum and planning experiences of the teacher. Instead, those topics which relate directly to policy-making and administrative responsibilities have been separated from the curriculum material, on the assumption that the administrator of a program already has had some preparation for and experience in classroom teaching.

The book is designed as a guide for those interested or involved in organizing a private nursery school, or directing a day care center, cooperative nursery school, or kindergarten. The materials were developed in the course of many years of experience in teaching young children, directing nursery schools, teaching both graduate and undergraduate students, and working with teachers and directors of day care centers, "Head Start," private schools, and cooperative schools in a supervisory capacity.

One of the purposes of the book is to help the reader become aware of factors in making administrative decisions. Toward that end, a variety of programs, both good and bad, have been evaluated, always with the well-being of the child in mind. Various approaches to administrative policies have been analyzed and alternatives discussed in order to provide a basis for intelligent decision-making.

Chapter 1 deals with the importance of early childhood education and provides information essential to answering some of the questions commonly asked about early childhood programs.

Chapter 2 gives an overall view of the different kinds of early childhood programs. Chapters 3 through 9 examine staffing, facilities, admission and grouping, health and safety, financing, records, and parent involvement. An equipment list and samples of records are included in the appendices.

My apologies to those who are sensitive about the use of masculine or feminine pronouns. In the interest of simplicity, certain conventions were followed. I hope that men will not be offended by the use of "she" to refer to the director and the teacher. The child has been referred to as "he," but no slight was intended to either sex.

A special acknowledgement is due the Educational Facilities Laboratories for permission to use the illustrations that appear throughout the book, particularly those in the chapter on facilities. I am indebted to my professional colleagues, my students, and many young children for the challenges and stimulation which led to writing this book. My appreciation goes to Jeri Wood and Sue Halstead, who typed the manuscript.

Contents

Early Childhood Education

1 | A Point of View About Early Childhood Education

FOR MANY YEARS, PSYCHOLOGISTS HAVE POINTED OUT THAT the first four or five years of a child's life is the period of most rapid growth and greatest susceptability to environmental influences. Early childhood educators have been equally outspoken regarding the need for early childhood programs to supplement the home experience of children between the ages of three and six years. However, adequate early childhood programs have been slow in coming. Day care and nursery school services have not developed fast enough to meet the growing demand, especially in deprived areas and in communities with a large population of working mothers.

Most early childhood educators admit that early childhood education is not a panacea; it cannot offer a guarantee for a child's future. What early childhood education can offer are positive experiences while enrolled in the program that will contribute to a child's growth and development and serve as a foundation for later school experiences. Despite extensive research in recent years, there are still controversies concerning what early childhood programs can and cannot do. Much of the antipathy towards, as well as support for, early childhood education lies in the realm of opinion. Many of those who support it have spent years observing and studying young children. Often such evidence is more observable than quantifiable, although through the years much data has been quantified. Some of this data will be summarized in this chapter as it relates to parent, teacher, or student of early childhood education.

INTELLECTUAL DEVELOPMENT

Good programs for young children are built on the conviction that during early childhood a base is formed for the abilities,

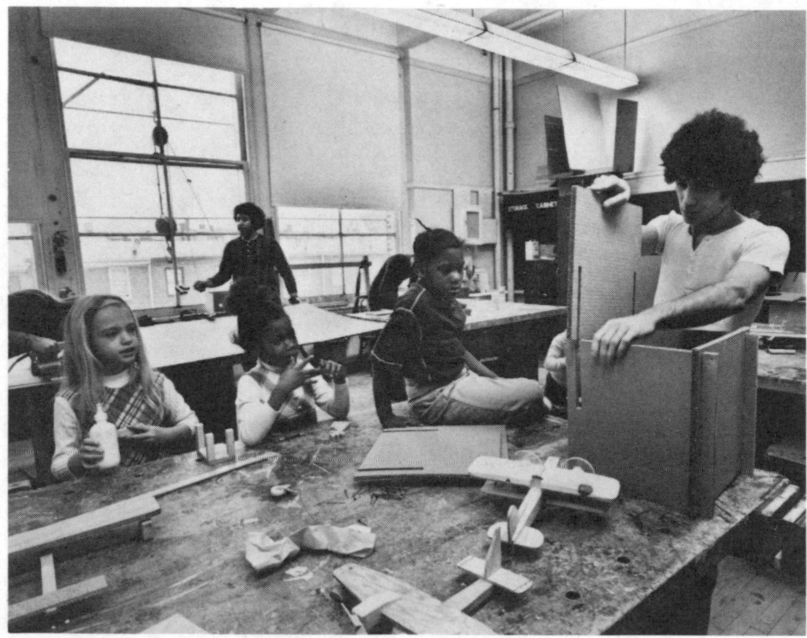

Courtesy of Educational Facilities Laboratories and George Zimbel

attitudes, interests, and values that will develop over a lifetime. Parents and teachers have observed how nursery schools and kindergartens have offered experiences capable of enriching the life of the young child. Despite the traditional notion that children younger than three years of age should be kept at home, it has been found that some children may be better off in a supplementary educational program. Current investigations show that some children grow up in such debilitating child-rearing environments that they may suffer lasting consequences.

Investigations indicate that the mental development of the infant and very young child may be particularly affected by dietary deficiencies.[1] In some cases poverty and malnutrition have been linked to intellectual underdevelopment in infants. Institutionalized children who are well fed and genetically normal but deprived of

1. Joe Frost and Billy Payne, "Hunger in America: Scope and Consequences," Nutrition and Intellectual Growth in Children (Washington, D.C.: Association for Childhood Education International, 1969), p. 9.

affection and stimulation at an early age may also show marked impairment in intellectual functioning.

The results of animal experimentation may have implications for early childhood education, although it is not known to what degree these findings are applicable to human development. Experiments by biochemists indicate that a rat placed in an intellectually enriched environment actually develops a brain with a heavier and thicker cortex, a better blood supply, and larger brain cells than a deprived animal. On the basis of his experiments, Krech[2] concluded that manipulating the educational and psychological environment induces long-lasting brain changes more effectively than direct administration of drugs. He indicated that educators probably change brain structure and chemistry to a greater degree than a biochemist could.

More evidence of the importance of stimulation in the early years comes from experimentation with infants. Hunt[3] and his associates have found that infants who have mobiles hung over their cribs at five weeks of age will learn to blink at objects by the age of 7 weeks on the average. Infants of mothers who agreed not to put anything on their cribs, however, failed to show this blink response until the age of 10.4 weeks on the average. It is not the mere development of these particular responses that is significant, but the implication that increases in the rate of development may be cumulative. "When such simple sensorimotor organizations are hastened in their development, they become available for coordination with others at this earliest age, and this allows these more complex organizations at a progressively earlier age."[4]

Central to any discussion of intellectual development in children is the controversy concerning the relative contributions of heredity and environment to intelligence. Fluctuation of opinion in this area has been a major factor in determining the credibility given to early childhood programs. The more it can be shown that a young child's surroundings can, in fact, improve intelligence, the more support is given to the concept of early childhood education.

2. David Krech, "Psychoneurobiochemeducation," *Phi Delta Kappan*, 50 (1969): 373.

3. Joseph McVicker Hunt, *The Challenge of Incompetence and Poverty* (Urbana: University of Illinois Press, 1969), p. 153.

4. *Ibid.*, pp. 153–154.

Unfortunately educators and psychologists are still far from understanding the exact nature of intelligence, and the debate continues. The reasonable approach for early childhood does not seem to be to discover whether biology or experience has the greater impact on intelligence but to define the relative significance of each and how the two factors interrelate.

Of the educators who hold opposing viewpoints, at one end of the continuum are those who believe that as long as a child is placed in a normal environment, he will naturally develop maximum intellectual potential. At the other extreme are those who believe that all differences in cognitive development are primarily due to experience.

Two of the most widely quoted sources supporting the latter view are Joseph McVicker Hunt's *Intelligence and Experience* and Benjamin S. Bloom's *Stability and Change in Human Characteristics.* These authors have been widely quoted to support the concept that early childhood programs expand opportunities for intellectual growth in children. In another publication, Hunt[5] indicates his belief that mankind has not yet developed a form of early childhood education which permits a child to achieve his full genetic potential. He feels that I.Q. can be boosted but that it will be at least two decades before there are adequate means of measuring such gains.

Bloom[6] sets out the reasons why the early environment is of crucial importance: it is the time of most rapid growth, it is the base upon which later development depends, and it is the time when learned behaviors are most lasting.

The most familiar work which has been used to support the position that intelligence is not fixed is Harold Skeels' study, which represents a twenty-one-year follow-up of the early studies by Skeels and Dye, and by Skodak in 1939. Skeels'[7] original experimental group consisted of 13 children in an orphanage, all under three years of age, with a mean I.Q. of 64. These children were so delayed in their development that no adoptive placement had been

5. Joseph McVicker Hunt, "Has Compensatory Education Failed? Has It Been Attempted?" Harvard Eduational Review, 39 (1969): 297.

6. Benjamin S. Bloom, *Stability and Change in Human Characteristics* (New York: Wiley, 1964), p. 215.

7. Harold Skeels, *Adult Status of Children with Contrasting Early Life Experiences*, Monograph of the Society for Research in Child Development, 31 (1966): 1–68.

found for them. The treatment consisted of placing the children in an institution for the mentally retarded under the care of the older female inmates. The children, who had been in an over-crowded ophanage with limited resources and staff, became the pride of the patients, who took over as mother-surrogates. Each mother-surrogate spent large amounts of time talking to, playing with, and training the child. The children also attended nursery school and kindergarten and were exposed to other kinds of enrichment experiences.

Skeels' contrast group was composed of twelve youngsters who were considered normal in mental development, but who were still in the orphanage at four years of age. The mean I.Q. when tested before they were two years of age was 86.7.

As soon as each child in the experimental group showed normal intelligence, as measured by intelligence tests and substantiated by qualitative observations, the experimental period was considered complete. Each child showed a gain of from 7 to 58 I.Q. points. The mental pattern for the children in the contrast group was quite the opposite. Losses were between 9 and 45 I.Q. points. In the first follow-up study, eleven of the thirteen children in the experiment were placed in adoptive homes. They now had a mean I.Q. of 95.9. The mean I.Q. of the contrast group was 66.1, a mean gain of 5.6 points over the last test of the experimental period.

Adult follow-up twenty years after the post-experimental follow-up provided striking contrasts. Skeels found that the mean grade completed by the experimental group was 12.8 while only one subject in the contrast group had an education beyond the eighth grade. Eleven of the thirteen experimental subjects had married and had a total of twenty-eight children who had a mean I.Q. of 103.9. None of the children showed any abnormality. In the contrast group only two men and none of the women had married. All members of the experimental group were self-supporting, with incomes within the average range. The incomes of the contrast group were markedly lower. The gains made in the experimental group were maintained, but the contrast group continued to show the adverse effects of their early environment.

PERSONALITY DEVELOPMENT

By the time the child enters his first preschool classroom he has had many experiences which are of profound significance for personality development. The self-picture of the child is fairly integrated by the third year of life. Once the concept of self has developed it becomes the evaluator, selector, judger, and organizer of future experience, and the child's behavior enhances and maintains his view. Personality is not fixed at age three, but the general view of the world and of oneself is already present. Possibilities for change are always present but the longer behavior persists the more difficult it is to change.

A study by Westman[8] contradicts the time-honored notion that children outgrow childhood behavior problems. Westman found that children who had adjustment problems in nursery school tended to have the same kind of adjustment problems in later school life. Low adjustment rating in nursery school correlated to later use of mental health services, and high adjustment rating corresponded to no later use of mental health services. Deviant family structure correlated with later family problems and non-deviant family structure correlated strongly with later academic achievement.

Much investigation has been focused on social behaviors such as aggression, imitation, sex identification, self-control, and dependency, providing information which is meaningful for early childhood programs. Aggression and dominance are the most salient kinds of social behavior during the preschool years. These traits are more frequent among advantaged children between the ages of four and one-half and five and one-half years than at any other age. This increase in aggressive and dominant behavior is accompanied by a parallel increase in friendly associations and contacts. Some investigators have viewed such behaviors as wholly negative or antisocial, but recent studies clarify that the preschool child who aggresses is frequently establishing new contacts by this behavior.

Many of the findings of Coopersmith[9] in his extensive study of the antecedents of self-esteem suggest important contributions which can be made by early childhood education. Coopersmith found that self-esteem is significantly associated with early childhood experience, parental characteristics, and parental attitudes and treatment. Adults who were high in self-esteem were less likely to

8. Jack Westman, "Nursery School Behavior and Later School Adjustment," *American Journal of Orthopsychiatry*, 37 (1967): 725–731.

9. Stanley Coopersmith, *The Antecedents of Self-Esteem* (San Francisco: W. H. Freeman Co., 1967).

have been loners in their childhood and more likely to have been close to their siblings and nonfamilial peers. Persons with high self-esteem had more frequent, positive, and congenial experiences during their childhood years.

It seems that a child's identity is influenced by the way he is treated, the opportunities provided for him, how he is evaluated as he copes with these opportunities, and how he perceives these evaluations. Children who are told that they are not good enough or smart enough tend to devalue themselves, which sets the stage for continued poor performance. For young children, negative self-views may be as damaging as physical illness or actual physical handicap. The building of self-esteem requires the combination of an emotional environment that tells the child he is loved and worthy, and a cognitive climate that allows him to be competent. Growth of self-esteem appears in the child's ever increasing awareness of his own autonomy. He begins to show more self-direction in his behavior. He has a clearer notion of his goals and how he wants to achieve them. If he cannot succeed in reaching his goals, he easily modifies them, or the method by which he intended to reach them.

A successful early childhood program teaches the child to like himself because he is worthy of being liked and because he can do things. It teaches him to like teachers because they like him and can help him. It teaches him to find pleasure in relationships with other children because he can trust them and is safe with them. Most importantly, it helps him to develop a positive self-image and to learn to function in social situations. Adults in the early childhood program can have an important role in assisting this development through their behavior towards the child and the setting they provide for social learning.

PHYSICAL DEVELOPMENT

Early childhood furnishes the same important basis for physical development that it provides for development in cognitive and affective areas. Until recently early childhood programs have tended to provide children with opportunities for muscle activity such as climbing, riding tricycles, and building with large blocks, without identification of specific values to be derived from them. At the other extreme some investigators have developed total programs which are highly reliant upon visual perception and fine motor activities. Perhaps neither is truly representative of the potential contribution to motor development, but these emphases have called attention to the relatedness of the psychomotor domain to the cognitive and affective domains. A factor which complicates the acquisition of data in this area is the view that all motor abilities are developmental. Data do not seem to contradict the developmental aspects of behavior; however, they do seem to support some differences in children which are attributable to experience.

The best predictor of large motor control in young children is a rating of muscle tone. Other factors such as physical conditions at birth, type of labor (natural or induced), specific learning opportunities, positive learning attitude and verbal ability are also related to the child's status. In areas such as copying and drawing there is an age-related improvement in ability although these abilities are still rather poorly developed at age five and training programs do not necessarily lead to significant improvement, particularly in children from the lowest socio-economic groups. Many children enrolled in Head Start groups continue to score low in these activities. Training activities with such children have been found to improve readiness but are not adequate to overcome the deficit in visual motor activities which exists at five years.

In discovering and treating the physical difficulties of children, the majority of early childhood programs have not had the proper staff or equipment. Health problems have often been found in conjunction with personality problems, neurological problems and mental retardation. Particularly in lower socio-economic levels it has not been uncommon to find children with major medical problems. Most frequently identified are dental diseases, nervous disorders, asthma and other allergic conditions, hemotologic diseases, gastrointestinal diseases, nutritional diseases, respiratory diseases, skin infections, enuresis, hernias, speech abnormalities, and vision and hearing losses.

Until recently, little had been done in early childhood programs to treat the health problems of young children, except in a few of the better day care programs. With the beginning of Project Head Start and federal government funding, however, a more comprehensive approach to the health problems of young children was taken. The findings of Head Start regarding the physical needs of children strongly underscore the need for a strong program of physical and mental health in connection with programs for young children. The programs instituted by Head Start in the area of health have been impressive. By March, 1967, two years after the Project was started, nearly 100,000 children had been treated for eye defects and 90,000 children had been treated for bone and joint disorders. Nearly 8,000 children were discovered to be mentally retarded and were referred for special training. Each child was discovered to have an average of five cavities. More than a million were immunized against measles and 740,000 children were immunized against polio.

Wherever child care and education are undertaken, adequate medical and dental attention must be assured. Psychological and health services are essential to the child's development and his later success in school.

GOALS

There are many differences of philosophy regarding the objectives of early childhood education and the implementation of educational programs. Wide differences exist in the goals of programs, the methods used, and the total orientation. Frequently, the differences in implementation are much greater than the philosophical differences in objectives. The emphasis varies from almost total direct instruction to a strong reliance on incidental learning, including a strong emphasis on the value of play in learning. Motivation also enters importantly into this difference, as many programs rely heavily on the child's desire to learn and explore, while others employ a highly complex system of rewards to effect modifications in the child's behavior in the direction of the goals of the program. Some programs strongly emphasize preparation for future school experiences. Such programs vary markedly from those which are more oriented toward present needs, assuming that optimal day-by-day experiences are the best preparation for the future.

The goals of an early childhood program will influence what kind of housing, staffing, and equipment will be needed, and other administrative decisions. It is therefore difficult to write a book that is equally applicable to all the conceivable kinds of program. This has not been attempted. The remainder of this section will attempt to present the point of view from which this book has been written.

The goals of a program must be clearly set forth before any educational program can be implemented. These objectives are related to all aspects of the child's affective or social and emotional development, physical and motor development, and cognitive or intellectual and language development. Objectives in these domains are highly interrelated and experiences which are provided in one area often contribute to growth in several areas. Cognitive learning has a very high degree of importance in defined objectives. But a broader definition is assumed than in programs which focus on pre-academic skills. Children learn from a wide variety of deliberately planned experiences as well as from incidental experiences, depending upon how well these experiences are guided by the teacher. Affective experiences, or learning connected with emotions and feelings, are no less significant than cognitive learning. Provision for the two are closely interwoven in curriculum planning. Children learn not only from the experiences which are provided for them by the teacher, but also from their interaction with each other and from their experimentation with a wide variety of materials.

Self-initiated play is the major vehicle for learning. In facilitating the child's learning through play, all kinds of materials can be used for encouraging self-expression and creativity. Through dramatic play, the child can work out emotional problems and prepare himself for adult roles. He can express the feelings and energies inherent in being a young child. If the teacher establishes interest centers in the room to which she continuously adds new materials, she should be able to stimulate the child's curiosity and to extend his learning. Such situations are planned and guided by the teacher but usually happen in the context of the child's responses and motives.

There are two kinds of group activities—those which the children choose to do and those planned and conducted by the teacher either for small groups of children or for the whole class. The small informal groupings which children form themselves are likely to have the highest degree of interaction and the highest social significance. The child soon learns that his continuous acceptance by this kind of group may demand a certain modification of his behavior and the teacher may need to intervene to help in the learning of socially acceptable behavior.

The teacher usually plans group activities such as discussions, stories, music and rhythmic activities for short periods of time. Such activities are not very frequent for the youngest children, as their attention span is very short. As the children get older and have had more experiences of this kind, they can participate for an increasing length of time. Such activities should be planned to bear some relationship to the self-selected activities of the children. Small-group instructional activities are also planned in order to give the children an opportunity to engage in experiments, manipulate materials, make observations, and engage in classification activities.

Children should be allowed a high degree of choice in the educational activities in which they engage, and they should have freedom to move from one activity to another. The teacher is active rather than passive. She makes suggestions to improve the child's activity; she asks questions which help the child's observations; she introduces new vocabulary and concepts. In short, she looks for opportunities to help the child gain as much as possible from the learning experience. Instructional goals are defined in terms of individual children and the individual guidance needed.

Children must be accepted as they are, whether they learn slowly or quickly, whether they come from the richest or the poorest homes, whether they are hostile and difficult to teach or are curious and eager to learn. This acceptance is essential to building a relationship with a child in which he is free to learn and to change his way of behaving. An essential part of this acceptance is planning a curriculum wherein children can be successful at the majority of activities while they are also challenged to further exploration. The child is encouraged to put forth real effort but is not expected to compete with other children. Activities have a definite relationship to the acquisition of academic skills, but such activities are always planned in terms of the child's immediate goals rather than from a predetermined adult-planned curriculum. In such a program, for example, some children may wish to engage in activities involving reading and writing skills, while others may not show this interest at all. What the latter child accomplishes is fully as important to his development as the accomplishment of the more academically advanced child. The atmosphere of the classroom must convey this message to him.

Cognitive Goals

Cognitive goals supply an important key to understanding the early childhood program. One interpretation of cognitive goals focuses on such skills as the recognition and classification of color, form, and shape and the ability to recognize certain likenesses and differences. Another interpretation emphasizes skills directly related to academic learning. The broader approach which is taken in this book recognizes cognition as involving both a content and a process of learning which are more inclusive in the child's broader encounters with his environment. This concept is of vast importance because it has many implications not only for the organization of the program and for the materials, but also for the kind of continuing guidance that is given to teachers by their supervisors and administrators. If the content to be taught is specifically identified and if the processes to be used can be specified, teaching is a much easier task than if the teacher makes random decisions regarding the selection of content, the guidance of children and use of materials. The approach to cognitive learning is a function of one's beliefs about how learning takes place.

The foremost goal of the early childhood program is to help the child become an intellectually emancipated human being for whom the learning process never ends. In today's world it is obviously impossible to prepare children for all the demands they will meet and for all the changes they will experience. We cannot possibly impart all the facts and skills they will need to learn. The problem is overwhelming unless we think of it in terms of helping today's children learn the motivations and skills to continue learning the rest of their lives.

The task is ultimately more difficult and more challenging than dealing with specifics. It is clearly focused on the development of the intellect—the critical, creative, and contemplative side of the mind. It rests firmly on the conviction that a high degree of trust can be placed in the powers of the individual to learn and that conditions or attitudes which interfere with learning should be removed. In short, the belief is that the child is a much more autonomous learner than many people think; that his learning is a continuous process, not limited to formal instruction and remedial efforts.

The process of teaching the child to learn involves helping him use sensory equipment such as vision, hearing, touch, and even smell and taste, to perceive the world around him and to use increasingly more complex processes to organize his perceptions. The school environment must include materials and activities which encourage the child to use these modalities to find out as much as he can about more and more things. It means that the teacher must be there to help the child express his experiences in words, to supply the needed vocabulary, and to express his observations in words.

The child must learn that there are many ways of acquiring information, but prior to that he must want "to know." The school acquaints the child with the tools of information gathering and situations in which he can use his newly gathered information. The blocks, the clay, the paint invite him to re-create the world as he has observed it; to incorporate his newly found concepts into the world as he has organized it. As he engages in this process, he encounters many problems which must be solved and many decisions which must be made. The teacher can help him acquire techniques which he can apply to many different problem-solving situations as he confronts them.

A further very important goal lies in the area of language development. Before entering school, children have a tremendous amount of experience with language. They have usually learned to speak with whatever sound system, grammar, and vocabulary they have heard most often at home. Some children have had an environment which provided many experiences and some have come from an environment offering meager opportunities. Some have come from homes where they talked primarily with adults while others have been indulged in baby talk or have had mostly opportunities to talk with other children. These differences in environment account for some of the differences in children's speech. Whatever their background and whatever abilities children have attained, the early childhood program will have as a primary objective the extension of their language abilities. Major emphasis will be on oral language abilities—learning to understand more complex structures and increasing vocabulary. This goal involves broadening the children's actual experiences and leading them to associate spoken language with the symbols which appear in pictures and print. These experiences should relate to the children in some personal way. This involves using materials from the children's everyday surroundings—signs, labels on food packages, television commercials, newspapers, and so on. Whatever the children respond to enthusiastically or ask questions about should be continued. Much can be learned in an atmosphere in which children's questions abound. These questions can provide a framework for learning.

The ability to form concepts constitutes a further cognitive goal. A recent study by Wann[10] pointed out a number of the abilities of young children in understanding and interpreting their physical and social environment. Children in this study were avid collectors of information and demonstrated a great range of knowledge. They also employed the essential elements of the process of concept formation. They associated ideas, attempted to discover cause and effect relationships, classified and generalized about the things they saw, heard, and felt in their environment. Because of their limited experience the conclusions reached by children are not always accurate. This means that care must be taken by the adult to help them grow in their ability to conceptualize accurately without seeming to convey a sense of disapproval at mistakes. Some misconceptions are allowed to pass unnoticed until children can make the observations which are necessary to correct the misunderstanding.

Certain intellectual factors are considered to contribute directly to creative power. The kind of thinking in which a variety of response is produced and in which the thinker allows himself to go off in different directions appears to be important to creativity. This is also true for the kind of intellectual activity represented in transformation, that is, changes of arrangement, organization, or meaning. A long list of other manifestations—the tendency to toy with ideas, to see patterns in data, the capacity to be puzzled, to sense ambiguities, or to discriminate have been associated with creative functioning through studies of creative individuals. The young child is quick to sense whether the situation invites him to

10. Wann et al., *Fostering Intellectual Development in Young Children* (New York: Bureau of Publications, Teachers College, 1962), p. 18.

use his imagination, to think of different responses from those of his classmates, or whether much the same behavior is expected of all children.

Affective Goals

Many early childhood education programs recognize that cognitive and affective experiences are interdependent. While the previous section focused on the growth of the mind as a powerful tool, this section will focus more on the building of the person. School experiences are important contributors to the child's cognitive growth, but they are no less important as contributors to the child's affective growth. We must appreciate the importance of mental development in the child's life and at the same time attend to the other aspects of emotional development which determine what kind of a person the child will be. The proper goal of education is not the production of intellectual paragons. Rather, it is the production of individuals who actualize themselves as human beings, given whatever intellectual potential they have.

Every child who is helped to develop a positive self-concept and who learns to function in social situations represents a valuable contribution to the total educational scene. This is a very important contribution that can be made by early childhood education.

For those children who have experiences that interfere with learning before entering preschool programs, the problem is one of changing attitudes and behaviors which have developed even before three or four years of age. It is particularly important for these children to feel that school is a place where they will be helped and accepted and where their integrity will be respected. All children need the freedom to be themselves, to be human. They must know what it is like to feel angry, anxious, happy, or sad, and that other people have these feelings too. In order to be sensitive to the world around him the child must be sensitive to his own feelings, sensitive to himself. He must have an openness to the world around him and the ability to interact with other human beings and to learn more about them.

Since the school plays an important role in the lives of the children it serves, it means that the school must provide an environment in which there is much interpersonal, spontaneous, coopera-

Courtesy of Educational Facilities Laboratories and Bob Perron

tive, action-oriented learning. The children must learn those attitudes and skills which will help them create for themselves that optimal relation between the expectancies of society and their own needs and demands. The everyday experiences of children must help them develop the resources for living amicably in society, in which there exist different ideas and points of view.

Psychomotor Goals

The preschool child's perceptual motor abilities are rather poorly developed compared to the abilities of older children. A child five years of age or younger may be quite poor at drawing or copying, while quite good at working puzzles or manipulating simple toys. He is able to profit from some types of training which may be made available to him but he does not profit from all kinds of experiences. Since children from disadvantaged backgrounds almost consistently lag behind more privileged children, there seems to be a very great need to provide these children with experiences in the psychomotor area. Whether such differences are linked to ability differences or whether they are largely a matter of opportunity and practice seems unclear. It does appear, however, that psychomotor development is linked to cognitive development. That is not to say that a program of psychomotor activities is the major factor in the development of reading ability, but that psychomotor experiences must be a primary part of preschool learning. The educational program should provide many opportunities for children to develop and practice these skills.

Goals for Health Care

With the exception of day care centers, most early childhood programs have felt that it is the parents' responsibility to provide for the physical and health needs of the children. But as more children from low socio-economic families are enrolled in programs, it has become necessary for the programs to become more comprehensive in their approach. Good health and nutrition are certainly important for every young child. This has important implications for early childhood education, since the relationship between nutrition and intellectual development in infancy and preschool years is well known. Medical problems must be identified and treated.

Involvement of Parents

Parental involvement in early childhood programs is another goal which will be more thoroughly discussed in Chapter 9. Objectives of most programs include the strengthening of ties between the child and his parents and assisting parents in providing a stimulating environment for children by exposing them to the kinds of activities that are enjoyable and instructive. Involved parents can also do a great deal to further their child's psychological development, by learning to become aware of the child's behavior patterns and understanding the behaviors that should be maintained and those that should be changed.

Parents should be encouraged to participate to the extent that the program allows or requires. Often early parental involvement can head off later conflict between home and school, particularly when several racial or ethnic groups are involved. Parent participation in advisory groups can help redefine the tasks that the program is attempting to accomplish and therefore reduce the potential conflict between home and school. Day care is also beginning to play a more active role in establishing the relationship between early childhood education and the home life of children.

VALUES

At the conclusion of an intensive search of the literature on values of early childhood education made in 1960, Fuller[11] concluded "the research support of values in early childhood education is abundant, but so is research support of weaknesses in present early childhood educational programs, of gaps in knowledge of how to measure what one wants to know, or confusion as to what value systems are to be employed when evaluations are made."

When an attempt is made to analyze the research on values in early childhood education, many difficulties are apparent. Programs are not truly comparable. For the most part, the programs evaluated in studies are not described, and little or no information is given about the goals of the program or of the curriculum. The methods used to evaluate a program present a particular problem. There are many tests which have been developed but which have not been adequately tried out on different populations of children. The test developed for one kind of program may not be well-suited for another kind of program. Since 1965 the preponderance of research has involved disadvantaged children; prior to that date few disadvantaged children were enrolled in the schools where research was conducted. Generalization from data collected in the varied programs is highly questionable. It is instructive, nevertheless, to know as much as possible about values in early childhood education and this section briefly reviews a range of studies.

Relationship Between Early School Experience and Intellectual Abilities

Most of the research planned specifically to determine the value of the education of disadvantaged children has placed a high

11. Elizabeth M. Fuller, *Values in Early Childhood Education* (Washington, D.C.: Department of Kindergarten-Primary Education, N.E.A., 1960), p. 62.

priority on cognitive development and has, therefore, relied heavily on the results of I.Q. tests such as the Stanford-Binet in evaluating the outcomes of the programs. These programs for disadvantaged children assume that the child's intellectual abilities are modifiable by the experiences that he has, and that if the quality of his experience can be changed, his I.Q. will reflect that change.

As early as the 1940's, there was a controversy over whether attending nursery school raised the child's I.Q. and this has never been completely resolved. As new programs began in the mid-1960's, researchers began to look with renewed interest at I.Q. gains as measurable evidence of the program's success, particularly in Head Start and other similar projects. Most Head Start programs, for example, produce an intellectual gain of five to ten points, but the results are by no means consistent. The longitudinal studies also show that gains tend to level off over a period of two or three years. Head Start and similar programs seem to help in stopping the progressive retardation of lower-income children, but do not close the gap between lower-income and middle-income children. Studies in which children in one type of curriculum are compared to those in another, such as a comparison of children enrolled in a Montessori School with a regular nursery school, do not show consistent long-range I.Q. gains in favor of any one type of program. The highly structured, cognitively oriented programs tend to show greater early gains, with children in the less structured programs catching up at about the third year of enrollment.

Relationship Between Early School Experience and School Achievement

One of the most important questions about early childhood education programs is the value which they have in future "pay off" in a child's achievement level in school. A related question is whether the children do better in first or second grade. The available data on programs today are very controversial. In most of the programs the results in terms of later school achievement tend to parallel the results in I.Q. changes. That is, the children tend to achieve better when they enter school than control children who have had no school experience, but within the next few years of school the control children tend to catch up with the experimental children. The children do not lose what they have gained through their earlier school experience but tend to level off to a plateau which allows other children to catch up with them.

In order to find out some of the factors influencing achievement gains from Head Start, a "Planned Variation"[12] study was planned through which some of the children were continuously enrolled in a program having similar objectives, from the time they entered Head Start at age three until they completed the equivalent of third grade. Preliminary results show that almost all children made significant gains in the areas of preacademic skills, but do not show any superiority of one curriculum approach over another. Results do show that the more complex curriculum models take more than a year to implement. Many aspects of these programs, in addition to their effect on school achievement, are being evaluated.

Interest in learning more about the relation of early childhood education to later school achievement began as early as the 1920's. Fuller[13] summarized fourteen studies which indicated some finding related to positive values of early childhood education, while only two found no positive values.

Morrison[14] found that more than eighty percent of the first grade pupils in those systems with kindergartens made normal or accelerated progress, as compared to only fifty-eight percent of the first graders in those systems without kindergartens. Teegarden[15] in 1932 found a conspicuous difference in favor of children with kindergarten experience in the industrial and middle-class districts, while the difference was only slightly in favor of the kindergarten children in the residential districts. Of the children in the study who failed, the non-kindergarten children tended to fail during the first semester, while the kindergarten children failed during the second semester.

12. Stanford Research Institute, *Implementation of Planned Variation in Head Start*, Interim Report, DHEW Pub. No. (OCD) 72–77, 1971.
13. Fuller, pp. 24–31.
14. J. Cayce Morrison, "The Influence of Kindergartens on the Age-Grade Progress of Pupils in New York's Elementary Schools," *Kindergarten Portfolio* (Washington, D.C.: Association for Childhood Education International, 1938), 4 pp.
15. Lorene Teegarden, "The Kindergarten and Reading Reversals," *Childhood Education* 9 (1932): 82–83.

Relationship Between Early School Attendance and Social Abilities

Studies in the area of social behavior are extremely difficult to relate to the problem of total school adjustment because most researchers examine single or multiple personality aspects instead of the overall picture of a child's adjustment. Fuller[16] summarized eleven studies that pointed out the relationships of early childhood education to later adjustment to school, and six studies of the effects of early childhood education on general social development. Though she drew no conclusion directly on the basis of these studies, she later concluded that the period of the 1920's and 1930's was characterized by the collection and interpretation of a vast array of normative data about child growth, development, learning, and adjustment. This was followed in the 1940's by much research interest in human needs and their effect on motivation. In the 1940's, with more small children available for study, interest was directed toward social living, group atmospheres, and group dynamics, which in turn focused attention upon personality and adjustment. These studies seemed to render early childhood education respectable. At that time, early childhood education was considered an acceptable program in facilitating the socialization of the child. Nursery school children were found to be less inhibited, more spontaneous, and more socialized after six months enrollment in a program. They were also found to have developed more independence, initiative, self-assertion, self-reliance, curiosity, and interest in the environment, as well as more habits of health and order.

Recent studies have not focused on the direct relationship between social behavior and school attendance. However, some of the Head Start studies have tested the assumption that children's learning is enhanced when they are happy, socially adjusted, and self-confident.[17] These findings revealed that children who had good peer relations were also able to play more freely and explore new environments with greater interest and curiosity. The study also showed that while children vary in cooperative behaviors, they are

16. Fuller, pp. 40–42.

17. Edith H. Grotberg, *Review of Research, 1965 to 1969* ERIC No. ED 028 308 (Washington, D.C.: Project Head Start, Office of Economic Opportunity, 1969), p. 18.

able to apply the principle of cooperativeness to new situations, when specifically taught the principle and the reasoning behind it.

In the study by Westman,[18] results supported the hypothesis that children who tended to have adjustment problems in nursery school also tended to have adjustment problems in later life, and the problems seemed to be of the same nature. Relations with peers in nursery school correlated strongly to later relations with peers.

One of the most interesting experiments in human relations was the Nursery in Cross-Cultural Education (NICE), studied by Lane and her associates.[19] This project was located in a San Francisco community subjected to the stresses of redevelopment. Children and their families came from three cultural milieus, a predominantly low-income Negro community, a low-income public housing community, and a middle-income group. The children were enrolled essentially as two-year-olds and remained in the project for three successive years. Specific goals for children included the development of a basic sense of trust, autonomy, initiative, cognitive development, and social competence. For adults in the enrolled families, representing several racial and ethnic groups, goals included growth in social competence, adaptability, and intergroup acceptance, as well as the families' expanded use of community resources and participation in community activities. The Lane study found that the children made significant gains in both intellectual ability and social competency. Social competency as measured here was related to cultural experiences and covered a wide range of behaviors such as "response to routine, response to the unfamiliar, following instructions, making explanations, sharing, helping others, initiating activities, giving direction to activities, reaction to frustration, and accepting limits." What was most important was that the children grew in all areas that were measured or observed. The implication of this finding is that a holistic approach to learning results in holistic gains. The authors attributed much of the success of the program to the family approach which was used in the development of the program, and the presence of socially competent models, both adult and peer.

18. Westman et al., pp. 725–731.

19. Mary B. Lane et al., *Nurseries in Cross-Cultural Education*, Final Report (San Francisco State College, School of Education: 1971), pp. 279–283.

Relationship Between Early School Experiences and Creativity

Very little has been written in the last few years about creativity in programs for young children. Margolin[20] worked with kindergarten children to test the hypothesis that if teachers encourage and praise differences in children's performance, the children will respond with a larger degree of difference than will children in a classroom where the teacher praises similar responses. Two public kindergarten classes were used as subjects, with one serving as the experimental group and one as the control group. Both groups were comparable in terms of I.Q., age range, and socio-economic background. Graduate students in art, in body movement, in poetry, and in creative dramatics worked with the experimental group for one-half hour per day during a semester. Children were made aware that the person working with them was working toward difference, not sameness. The test for body movement expression indicated that the children in the experimental group used more levels of space in their ideas, used more parts of their body, and varied their pace to greater degrees than the control group. In the area of graphic arts, the experimental children used all the different kinds of media, while the children in the control group went only to large sheets of newsprint, just one of many possibilities.

Torrance[21] described a program called the "Creative-Aesthetic Approach" in which activities were carefully planned to encourage creative thinking, problem solving, fluency of ideas, verbal expression, and auditory and visual discrimination. Children were urged to offer ideas freely, to hazard guesses, and to try to predict possible outcomes. The experimental group of twenty-four kindergarten children made significant gains over the control group on verbal measures, figural originality, and total figure creativity. They were also superior on all verbal creativity measures and on all the originality measures. On the basis of this and other experimentation,

20. Edythe Margolin, "Conservation of Self-Expression and Aesthetic Sensitivity in Young Children," *Young Children*, 23 (1968): 155–160.

21. E. Paul Torrance et al., *The Creative-Aesthetic Approach to School Readiness and Measured Creative Growth*, ERIC No. ED 017 344 (Athens: University of Georgia, Research and Development Center in Educational Stimulation, 1967), 15 pp.

Torrance[22] concludes that many children needlessly sacrifice their creativity due to the rigidly structured situation in most schools. He believes that creative thinking and the production of new ideas can be taught, and that such learning should not be left to chance.

According to Starkweather,[23] the value that may be derived from an increased understanding of creative ability in the preschool years depends on whether our role in training children is seen as that of teaching by authority or setting the stage for creative learning. While she is willing to admit that we must do both (some things must be learned by authority), in those situations in which a child must learn creatively it is necessary to free him for that learning. Starkweather feels that as our understanding of creative ability increases, we should be able to provide children with the experiences necessary for creativity. Studies suggest that we could cultivate creativity if we really valued it as an outcome of education.

PROVIDING EARLY CHILDHOOD EDUCATION

Early childhood education has been poorly understood by the general public throughout the years. Many parents want and expect something from early childhood education that it has not been able to guarantee: an assurance that children will be more successful in later school experiences if they are enrolled in preschool programs. Yet this has not kept many parents who are convinced that education is beneficial to their children from finding ways to provide programs for their children. Perhaps a factor which is influential is that early childhood education has never been provided in many areas of the country. Parents who did not have the opportunities for early childhood education themselves often do not feel the necessity of it for their children. Many other parents believe that children below the age of six belong at home with their mothers. People in rural areas have argued against early childhood education because of the distance the children would have to travel to reach school. Statistics show, however, that when kindergartens are

22. E. Paul Torrance, "Must Creative Development be Left to Chance?" in *Creativity: Its Educational Implications*, ed. John C. Gowan et al. (New York: Wiley, 1967), pp. 96–101.

23. Elizabeth Starkweather, *Potential Creative Ability and the Preschool Child*, ERIC No. ED 109 900 (Stillwater: Oklahoma State University, 1966), 9 pp.

provided in rural areas, almost as many children enter school at age five as enter at age six.

One of the major reasons for the lack of public support is the problem of financing. Citizens are reluctant to appropriate funding that would mean a rise in taxes. Many citizens either do not have children of preschool age or do not think that early childhood education is important enough to pay for it. As most school systems are plagued with financial problems, early childhood education faces an uncertain future in school-budgeting priorities.

Defining and Maintaining Standards

Maintaining high standards for educational programs provided for children has been a constant concern of professional organizations and others interested in promoting the welfare of children. The concern is for both the health and safety of the children and for the educational program that is provided. Not only are uniform standards nonexistent, but some areas permit any individual who feels like it to open a school or day care center in his home or garage. Parents, often unaware of the dangers, or in desperate need of someone to care for their children, enroll their children in places they have never seen. If all such centers were required to meet minimum standards in safety, health, and staff qualifications, the first steps would have been taken to eliminate the exploitation of children.

In order to insure at least minimum standards in programs which receive federal support under such acts as the Social Security Act, the Economic Opportunity Act, or the Manpower Development and Training Act, the White House requested the establishment of the Federal Panel on Early Childhood Education, which issued a statement of *Federal Interagency Day Care Requirements*. These requirements cover all day care programs and facilities utilized by the administering agencies which receive federal funds, whether facilities are operated directly by the administering agencies or are contracted to other agencies. Such programs and facilities must also be licensed or meet the standards of licensing applicable in the state in which they are operated.[24]

24. Federal Panel on Early Childhood, *Federal Interagency Day Care Requirements, Pursuant to Se. 522(d) of the Economic Opportunity Act*, ERIC No. ED 026 145 (Washington, D.C.: Government Printing Office, 1968).

The provision that all programs must meet minimum standards does not guarantee that every program will be a good one. There is a considerable gap between a bare minimum standard and a program of highest quality. Minimum standards merely provide a safeguard and do not assure a high-quality program.

Developing Qualified Staff

The rapid growth of early childhood programs has created a great shortage of qualified teachers. There simply has not been the demand over a long period of years, and teacher education institutions have been slow to respond to the current need. This shortage also exists in part because private schools have not been able to offer salaries adequate to attract qualified personnel.

Qualified staff are needed at all professional levels and at para-professional levels. In college and university education programs, it is difficult to find faculty who have both competence with young children and the required educational background. There are also few professionals at the state or local supervisory level. Although the majority of kindergarten programs in some states are staffed by certified teachers, many local private nursery schools, day care programs, and Head Start programs are not directed by persons who have completed a college curriculum in child development or early childhood education, and such programs often do not have fully qualified teachers on their staffs.

High Costs of Operating Quality Programs

Programs for young children are costly, particularly comprehensive programs of day care, estimated to cost from $2,000 to $3,000 per child per year.[25] This is more than most families in the income levels between $5,000 and $15,000 per year can afford, yet such families are not eligible for programs such as Head Start. If a mother is working, she is almost forced to turn to inferior programs for her children.

Because of the need for small classes and the need for a

25. Mary D. Keyserling, "Day Care: Crisis and Challenge," *Childhood Education*, 48 (1971): 62.

small child-teacher ratio, the costs of early childhood education exceed the costs for the education of older children. Good early childhood programs should be available to those children whose families desire them and at a price they can afford. This means that some programs will have to be subsidized to a considerable degree.

Coordinating Services and Programs for Children

Early childhood programs are financed in many ways, some privately supported by endowments and philanthropic sources, and some publicly supported by state and federal funds. Partly because of this and partly because there are no local coordination agencies, there is much fragmentation and duplication of services. Thus far, little has been done to coordinate all of these programs, each of which is unique in terms of the population reached or the service provided. Plans for the coordination of federally funded programs are in the beginning stages. The legislative mandates of the Economic Opportunity Amendments of 1967 require that the Secretary of Health, Education, and Welfare and the Director of the Office of Economic Opportunity coordinate programs under their jurisdictions which provide day care. The purpose is to establish common standards and regulations and mechanisms for coordination at state and local levels. This has resulted in the development of the *Federal Interagency Day Care Requirements* previously referred to and the organization of Coordinated Child Care Committees (4-C) whose responsibility it is to work on the state and local levels. They coordinate community services available to children and design programs involving the complex relationships which result when the educator is concerned with health matters, the nurse with social service activities, and the parent-coordinator with helping professionals. This program does not as yet provide funds to a community, but it is a means by which a community may be better able to utilize available funds.

Continuity Between Early Childhood and School Programs

As a general rule, there is no plan for continuity between the program for children under five years of age and public school programs. Most public schools make little attempt to find out what previous school experiences a child has had or to build on these experiences. There is usually very little difference in the treatment of a child who has two or three years of nursery school and the child who has had no prior school experience at all. In programs where there is true individualization of instruction, this may not be of great importance as far as the child's progress in school is concerned. Those teachers who have worked with the child during his earlier years should be able to supply some valuable and helpful information about the child and the experiences he has had, which would enable the current teacher to meet his needs better. It often happens that the programs in which a child is enrolled over a period of his preschool and primary years have conflicting purposes. These discontinuities which are experienced make for difficulties which should not be allowed to develop.

A year or two of preschool education should call for an examination of the school years that follow, because every year thereafter will be affected. This examination should raise questions about curriculum and ways teachers can organize the classroom to allow for the differences between children. With the addition of kindergarten to a school system, the establishment of a working relationship with local nursery schools could provide the occasion to initiate long-needed change and to cultivate sensitivity to every child.

Early childhood education is making progress, despite the problems. More and more states are providing kindergartens in public schools and more children are enrolled in day care programs that are licensed. Progress is slow but current interest is high and so is hope for the future.

QUESTIONS FOR DISCUSSION

1. What do you believe are the essential characteristics of a good early childhood program?

2. Talk with three parents who have children who are enrolled in an early childhood program and with three parents who have not enrolled their children in a program. What are the reasons they give for enrolling or not enrolling their children? What do the parents expect of the program?

3. What is the most important contribution you believe early childhood education can make in the life of a child?

4. What are the requirements for operating a nursery school program in your state or community? For operating a day care center?

2 Diversity in Early Childhood Programs

WE HAVE HAD EARLY CHILDHOOD PROGRAMS IN THIS COUNTRY for a long time. Kindergartens were started well over a hundred years ago, and nursery schools have been around for almost half a century. Still, there is considerable confusion as to what constitutes an early childhood program. Part of this confusion may be due to the fact that public school kindergartens are the only early childhood programs formally associated with public school systems. So many other programs have grown up in response to such a variety of needs that their functions and services are not always understood. Some programs for young children are designated as nursery schools yet do not have an educational program. Other programs call themselves child care or day care centers but actually carry on a strong program. During the last few years, with the increasing demand for day care services, the situation has become even more complex. All kinds of cooperative arrangements have been made among parents for the care of their children, frequently without professional consultants or qualified teachers. Federally funded programs have also added to the confusion by introducing new nomenclature such as "Child Development Centers" to apply specifically to Head Start programs.

Not only is there the problem of telling an "educational" program from a "non-educational" program, but also of assessing what the teaching objectives of any given program will be. For example, a program which claims to emphasize academic skills may not do so at all, since it may have no one on the staff qualified to teach academic skills to young children.

WHAT IS A "SCHOOL"?

Early childhood programs may be classified according to the age level of the children they serve, and according to their functions, such as a laboratory school, or a day care school. Kindergartens are generally for five-year-olds, and nursery schools for three and four-year-olds. This is an easy distinction to make, as most kindergartens are located in the public schools and nursery schools are financed by other means. In areas where there are no kindergartens in the public schools, a kindergarten facility may include both four and five-year-old children but rarely three-year-old children. A day care center typically cares for nursery school children during school hours and frequently takes kindergarten and older children after their school hours. A laboratory school may be either a nursery school or kindergarten. Again, it is unlikely to be a kindergarten in an area where kindergartens are a part of the public school, unless the laboratory school also enrolls children of elementary school ages. Parent cooperative groups are usually nursery schools in communities that have public kindergartens, but nursery school and kindergarten groups in communities that do not.

As the number of early childhood programs continues to expand, so does their variety. Many early childhood programs have developed in response to the particular needs of the community and the desire of families to enrich both their own lives and those of their children. It is necessary for a program to have an educational focus to be legitimately called a school.

WAYS PROGRAMS DIFFER

Goals

Programs vary as much in goals, organization and philosophy as they do in size, shape and location. There are curriculums, for example, in which some programs emphasize cognitive learning experiences while other programs focus on affective and psychomotor experiences. A program may be planned as an enrichment experience or as a compensatory experience for deprived children, in which there is a deliberate attempt in the curriculum to compensate for educational deficiencies.

In addition to curriculum differences schools vary in the nature of parent participation. Cooperative nursery schools will usually include comprehensive parent education goals, which extend far beyond the children's daily school program.

No matter what type a program is, its individual characteristics and overall philosophy will be crucial in determining the roles of teachers and administrators.

Administrative Organization

The administrative organization of early childhood programs ranges from the small private school with an owner/director and an assistant teacher, to a program enrolling several hundred children and employing a large staff functioning under an administrator and a board of directors.

The organizational plan for most nursery schools and kindergartens outside the public school is usually relatively simple, consisting of a director and a professional and nonprofessional staff.

Admission Policies

Admission policies are related to the overall goals of the program. Some programs have no further purpose than providing a good educational program for the children. Such programs are likely to have a first-come-first-serve policy and maintain a waiting list for children who did not apply soon enough to be admitted. Such programs do not usually specify any particular obligations of parents toward the school. If the school is a parent cooperative, however, admission of the child will be contingent upon the parent's willingness to take an active role in the activities of the school. Programs financed by federal funds may enroll only children from low-income families. Enrollment policies often play an important part in determining what kind of educational program is available to any given child in a community.

Financing

The lack of financing from any consistent source is one of the most significant reasons for the diversity of programs in early childhood education. As public schools have not generally established programs for children younger than five years of age, programs have been forced to find other means of funding. Most early childhood programs are supported through the payment of tuition or through the payment of tuition combined with the contribution of services. Because local groups have usually had to find their own sources of funding for early childhood programs, the programs have frequently reflected a specific purpose or a specific community need. Financing has always been a problem because good programs for young children are expensive to operate, compared to programs for older children.

Parent Involvement

In cooperative nursery schools and Project Head Start, parent involvement is an intrinsic part of the educational program of the children. Parent education in other types of programs has usually been on a very limited basis, with parents relatively uninvolved in the activities or organization of the schools. Many schools have almost held themselves apart from the parents, providing only some kind of report card and an occasional conference when problems arise. These extremes account for different kinds of parent attitudes towards programs.

Location

One of the most important aspects of early childhood programs is their location. Schools occupy a unique position in our society and have for many years served the communities in which they are located. But since kindergartens comprise the only early childhood programs housed in public schools, for the most part early childhood programs have not been included in the community in the same way.

Programs may be housed in any facility which would serve the purpose reasonably well. This includes stores, community centers, church schools and family homes. Often the space is used for many purposes, necessitating the removal of much of the equipment during the evening when other groups meet. The search for suitable facilities or the struggle to make facilities usable has often been the means of developing a real spirit of community among the school staff and parents.

Location of suitable facilities often creates the related problem of providing transportation. Ideally, parents would live near early childhood programs and would be able to take their own children to school. If no suitable space can be located which is convenient, children must be transported to the program. Parents in middle-income groups may be able to deal with the problem, but parents of low-income families frequently cannot cope with this problem. It then becomes a function of the school to provide the transportation in much the same way that public school provides transportation, which may necessitate additional expense and sometimes complicated arrangements.

GOVERNMENT SUPPORT OF EARLY CHILDHOOD PROGRAMS

Almost all states now have legislation permitting the establishment of public school kindergartens. This does not mean that almost all children have the opportunity to attend public school kindergarten, since only thirty-five of the states have legislation providing state aid for these kindergartens.[1] The number of public school kindergartens has increased, particularly during the last five years, but services are still limited. Several states that give state aid to kindergartens have many schools that do not actually have kindergartens. This is typical of states which have only recently begun to provide state aid.

Support for nursery schools is considerably less. Approximately one-fourth of the states have legislation authorizing local boards of education to use local funds for prekindergarten children.[2] Six states provide some kind of support to prekindergarten programs. At least twenty-six states offer some other state-supported services to children younger than six, such as medical and dental care, nutritional programs or special programs for the handicapped.[3]

1. Education Commission of the States Task Force in Early Childhood Education, *Early Childhood Development: Alternatives for Program Implementation* (Denver: Education Commission of the States, 1971), pp. 84–92.
2. National Council of State Consultants in Elementary Education, p. 21.
3. Education Commission of the States Task Force on Early Childhood Education, p. 81.

The State Department of Education is the agency responsible for kindergarten programs in thirty-seven states and is responsible for prekindergarten programs in six states. In states where the responsibility for prekindergarten programs is not delegated solely to the State Department of Education, it is delegated to the State Department of Welfare or of Social Services or of Health or is shared by one of these agencies.[4]

In over one-third of the states legislation provides for mandatory or voluntary registration, licensing, or accreditation of nonpublic nursery schools and/or kindergartens by the state education department.[5] This leaves a large number of states in which nonpublic schools are neither accredited nor subject to state controls. In some states it is possible for anyone to open a so-called "school for young children."

A larger percentage of states have legislation which requires the licensing of day care centers or day nurseries. These programs tend to be the ones which are administered under the department of social welfare or social services. These departments often have worked out excellent standards and provide helpful consultant services.

State legislation could do much to raise the standards of early childhood programs. States could require that local boards of education provide school opportunities for all five-year-olds, and for three and four-year-old children whose parents want them to attend at local expense. Private schools could be brought under state supervision if state departments of education were to require the registration of all groups enrolling children under six years of age. Consultative services and guidelines for local programs could be authorized by the state education department, which should also develop acceptable standards of operation for these services. Some equalization of opportunities could be effected by providing state financial support in rural and urban communities where local funds are inadequate.

One cannot assume that the enactment of legislation is the cure for all the ills that affect the education of young children. The fact that a program is permitted by law does not guarantee that it

4. Education Commission of the States Task Force on Early Childhood Education, p. 82.
5. National Council of State Consultants in Elementary Education, p. 21.

will be established. Improvement in laws results in better school services and facilities only to the degree that educators and parents cooperate to make the best use of the services. It is necessary to remove the legal obstructions to good education, but it is also necessary to develop community understanding of good programs.

Legislating and implementing minimal standards for early childhood programs is difficult. Standards must be developed which foster and protect the education and experiences of young children. Such standards must be flexible enough to encourage research and program innovations; standards which are too rigid may arouse such resistance that practitioners will reject them. Many feel that it is better to set reasonable minimum standards and administer the standards in a way that permits schools to meet all the requirements over a period of several years.

Continuing consultation is an important part of the development and attainment of any standards for programs for young children. Presumably, if standards are administered by the state department of education, consultant services would be provided by that agency. Each school should have a direct and continuing relationship with the same consultant so that there is a consistency in the recommendations which are made and the inservice opportunities which are planned. Standards are successful only when they provide schools with the guidance to plan and improve their own potential for attaining the highest quality of education.

TYPES OF EARLY CHILDHOOD PROGRAMS

In order to provide an understanding of different early childhood programs as they exist today, it is important to set forth some of the characteristics which constitute the different programs. Any teacher who plans to accept an early childhood education position, or any parent who plans to enroll a child in an early childhood program, will benefit from general knowledge of the various programs. Each parent will need to make some kind of judgment regarding the appropriateness of the program for the needs of the child and the family. A wisely made and informed decision can make the difference between an exciting and worthwhile experience and a negative, discouraging experience.

Private Schools

Private schools are supported entirely, or almost entirely, by fees. For this reason private schools tend to be expensive and affordable only by families with adequate financial resources. Private schools often provide transportation to and from school or recommend a driver with whom the parent may send the child. They may also provide extra services for parents who have a large number of professional responsibilities, club or social activities, or other personal interests.

A private school may be a small enterprise, organized and taught by an owner/director and offering one or two classes daily, or a large profit-making organization with a large professional staff teaching several groups of children daily. The owner or director may have no professional qualifications in early childhood education and may rely on staff members to give leadership to the educational program. This type of private school might include elementary and possibly secondary school, as well as an early childhood program. Some children may attend only for their early childhood years, while others continue on through elementary or high school.

There is little uniformiy of goals in the programs of private schools. In some areas private schools have developed because of dissatisfaction with the existing system of public education, in which case the program is likely to reflect this dissatisfaction. Where schools are felt to be too rigid and formal, the more "open" and informal programs are likely to develop. Where schools are considered inadequate in academic areas, a more academic program is likely to emerge.

Admission to private school is usually by application, and there may be a waiting list if the school is very popular. Admission policies may be more flexible than in public schools, so that a child may be accepted at an earlier age than in public school. There may also be considerable adaptability in the number of days per week that the child is enrolled. Such programs may be specifically designed to serve the needs and wishes of the parents.

Parent education activities are likely to be given relatively little emphasis. While the programs of some private schools include parent education meetings and regularly scheduled conferences, other private schools have only casual contact with the parents. These schools may welcome parental involvement, though it is seldom a condition of enrollment.

Some private schools have facilities constructed especially for their purpose. Estates and large homes have been converted into schools, with beautiful settings and expansive grounds. Other private schools may be housed in homes which have had minor renovations to make them suitable for school use.

Parent Cooperative Nursery Schools and Kindergartens

The parent cooperative nursery school and kindergarten have become increasingly popular in the last twenty years, particularly in areas where there had been no kindergartens available. Cooperative schools are seldom provided for just one age level. In areas which lack kindergartens, cooperative schools are usually for four and five-year-olds, and in areas which have kindergartens, cooperative schools are usually for three and four-year-olds. Part of the reason for this kind of arrangement is to provide continuity of leadership. The parents of the youngest children one year are able to move into the leadership positions the second year, thus maintaining continuous administration and organization.

Cooperative nursery schools have the dual purpose of providing a good educational experience for both the children and the parents. Families who wish to share the preschool experiences of their children often help organize or affiliate with a cooperative nursery school. The school may operate under a constitution which defines the role of the parents and the role of the professionals, so that both share in the educational responsibilities. Policy is made by a board consisting of officers and committee chairmen. Parents usually assume responsibility for such activities as assisting the teacher in the classroom, working out the participation schedule, enrolling the children, purchasing supplies and equipment, maintaining equipment, and collecting tuition and other fees. Though they assist the teacher in implementing and planning the program, the major responsibiilty for curriculum and teaching falls to the director and the teachers.

Through participation in the program, parents are able to provide their children with a regularly supervised educational program planned under the direction of a professional educator. They are able to provide their children with a wealth of educational activities, companionable playmates and more equipment than any home could provide. They have a voice in determining how the cooperative operates and just what parent education activities are provided. They also have some free mornings or afternoons to pursue their own interests.

Cooperative schools are maximally effective if at least two groups of children are involved and minimally effective if they become larger than about six groups. When the number of parents involved becomes too large, parents begin to lose some of the feeling of personal responsibility. When the size of the group is too small, financing is difficult and continuity of leadership is difficult to maintain.

Admission to parent cooperatives is usually based on the age of the child and the willingness of parents to assume specifically designated responsibilities. Sometimes a provision is made to give preference to families which have previously been affiliated with the school. Enrollment is continuous from one year to the next, as long as the family wishes to be involved. Most of the mothers in the cooperative school are either not employed or employed only on a part-time basis. Most working mothers do not have the time needed to devote to a cooperative.

Cooperatives usually are not selective in admission and welcome children from all socio-economic groups. Some cooperatives include families with handicapped children, feeling that the experience will be worthwhile to all the children involved.

Parent education activities are varied. Some schools have complex orientation periods for new parents; some have regular discussion groups conducted on a class basis by the teacher. Cooperative schools hold regular parent meetings which involve both business sessions and educational experiences. Conferences with the child's teacher are also a regular aspect of the program.

Financing is largely from fees and tuition, which are based on actual operating costs. Cooperative schools are nonprofit in the sense that they do not plan to make money and frequently do not maintain large amounts of money in their treasury from one year to the next. Fund raising projects may supply additional operating funds. Projects such as bake sales, rummage sales, or benefit card parties may be planned and conducted by the group to provide money for special purchases. A special library fee may be charged at regular intervals to be used to buy books or library equipment. Major expenditures usually require board action, so that both the director and the parents have a part in the financial operation of the school.

Finding adequate facilities is frequently a major problem, as relatively few cooperatives are financially able to own or build their own facilities. A cooperative nursery school may utilize rented facilities from a church during the week. This may involve a sharing arrangement whereby the cooperative uses some of the church's space and equipment during the week, and the church uses some of the cooperative's equipment for the church-school program on Sunday. Although such schools have no religious affiliation, the churches often see this use of their facilities as a contribution to the life of the community.

Church-Sponsored Nursery Schools and Kindergartens

Many churches have organized nursery schools and kindergartens as a part of their religious education program, often in response to the interest of young families in the church membership. The church-sponsored school has been particularly popular in communities that have no public school kindergartens. A church-sponsored school may be operated by the church and directed by members of the church ministry. It may also be run on a cooperative basis with a parent board and parent participation. This is similar to a cooperative school, except that a member of the church governing board may serve on the school board to maintain liaison between the school and the activities of the church.

Increasingly, church governing boards are recognizing the advantages of schools for young children in fostering religious values. The school benefits the community and benefits the church directly by sharing the Sunday school equipment needed by both groups. It is possible that in the future, more and more young families will be able to look to their church or synagogue to provide daily educational programs.

The church-sponsored school usually has policies regarding

admission made by its own board, subject to approval by the governing board of the church. These policies may limit enrollment to the families holding membership in the church or they may give preference to families holding membership in the church, particularly if there is a shortage of early childhood educational programs in the community. Policies regarding enrollment, however, may give no preference on the basis of church membership, with a first-come-first-serve policy for anyone in the community interested in enrolling a child in the school program.

The educational program of the church-sponsored school will reflect the religious teachings of the church in varying degrees. Some will observe some of the rituals of the church. Others will not even require that the teachers have the same religious beliefs as those of the church, and the school program will differ little if at all from other early childhood programs. The policy of the school will be of particular interest to prospective teachers and parents.

The attitudes of church boards toward early childhood programs may differ widely. At worst, some members of the board may oppose the school and will give minimal support. At best, the church may assume part of the cost of operating the school. Such contributions as maintenance, custodial costs, or the use of facilities without rent can be of great assistance in the financing of a school. The fees are likely to be less than those of a private school. Depending on the amount of support provided by the church, the fees may be comparable to other cooperative schools, if the school is a cooperative.

One of the real advantages of the church-sponsored school lies in the mutual use of the facilities by both school and church. Churches seeing the advantages of providing a nursery school or kindergarten are building facilities which are suitable for the purpose. Often the school facilities are needed for the church school but are difficult to justify acquiring for use for only one day a week.

Child Development Centers or Project Head Start

Child Development Centers, better known as Project Head Start, are the first federally supported educational program for children under six years of age. Previous government support has been for providing day care in order to permit parents to work or provide employment for unemployed teachers. Child Development Centers were started in 1965 as part of the War on Poverty and have been continued under the Office of Child Development.

The Child Development Center is both a concept and a community facility. It represents the drawing together of all those resources—family, community and professional—which can contribute to the child's total development. As a community facility, it is organized around its classroom and outdoor play areas. It provides a program for health services, meals, and parent interviews and counseling.[6]

The comprehensive program is designed to help the very poorest children in ways that will not only improve their chances for school success, but also enhance the total growth and development of their families.

Project Head Start programs are organized and conducted under locally organized Community Action Boards which are made up of representatives of local community agencies and elected representatives of the target areas to be served by the Board. Project Head Start also has its own advisory board which is made up of parents served by the program, and representatives of educational and community agencies. This Board is responsible for many of the policy decisions regarding Project Head Start.

Money for Head Start programs comes largely from federal grants. In order to be eligible for this grant, a community must contribute twenty percent of the cost of the program either in funds or in "in-kind" contributions, such as consultant services, volunteer services or rent-free facilities. There is no charge to the child who attends. The service includes transportation to and from the center if needed. Children who are enrolled in Head Start must come from families whose income is below the poverty line, which is a sliding scale depending on both income and the number of children in the family. A small percentage of children, not more than ten percent, may come from families which do not meet these criteria. With more and more families aware of the program, fewer children are enrolled who do not meet the criteria, and those who are enrolled

6. Office of Economic Opportunity, *Project Head Start, Daily Program I for a Child Development Center* (Washington, D.C.: U.S. Government Printing Office, 1967), p. 1.

are apt to have problems which indicate a need for the program. Recent guidelines require admission of handicapped children. The goal of Head Start is to serve all eligible families in the community. The ability to do this, however, is based on the availability of funds, and finding families who need and want to participate in the program.

Guidelines for Project Head Start include standards regulating staffing and the size of class groups. These guidelines call for a teacher, a paid aide, and a volunteer for each group of fifteen children. Parents are encouraged to serve as aides and volunteers. Where they have been involved in training programs designed for career development, some parents have been able to move into teaching positions, and teachers have been able to move into the position of director. Some experience in working with low-income populations is considered essential to obtaining a teaching position in Head Start.

Head Start programs are housed as close as possible to the areas from which the children come. The programs take place in churches, community centers, and storefronts. They utilize almost any kind of facility which provides adequate space usable on a daily basis.

Experiences provided for the children are varied. Much emphasis is placed on the development of language and self-concept. Children are given a wide variety of experiences designed to extend their knowledge of the world around them and of the community in which they live. All programs provide at least one full meal per day, usually lunch; some programs may provide fruit juice and cereal upon arrival in the morning, for children who have not had any breakfast. Snacks are also provided at midmorning and midafternoon. Some programs have the same hours as day care programs, but most are in operation for about four hours a day, beginning in the morning and continuing until after the lunch hour.

Every Project Head Start program carries out a program of parent activities; parents serve on advisory boards, help in the classrooms, and decide on staff and policies related to the program. Providing any assistance which is practical is more important than trying to interest parents in one specific program. Helping the parent to contribute to the community is an important goal of Project Head Start.

Day Care Centers

Day care centers provide full day care for children whose parents work or are incapable of caring for them full time. Besides offering an enriching educational experience for the child, day care includes comprehensive social and medical services. Programs which receive federal funds are required to provide such services by the Federal Interagency Guidelines. Since federal funds are available only for programs which serve low-income families, these guidelines usually apply to families in greatest need of the services. Licensing is required in most states and is generally done by departments of social welfare. The most significant support also comes from social security legislation administered by welfare departments.

Day care centers have increased in number over the last few years from about 250 thousand in 1965 to approximately 700 thousand in 1971.[7] The number of children under six years of age with working mothers has risen by about two million since 1965. Many of the licensed centers which have been added have been subsidized by public funds and are therefore available only to very poor families. Few families in which both parents work are eligible for subsidized day care. Two groups of children are in urgent need of day care. The first is comprised of children of employed mothers who must arrange for satisfactory full day care, and the second group are children from economically deprived families who cannot provide adequate care.

A day care center is most frequently administered by a governing board which may be an incorporated or an unincorporated group. It is the responsibility of this board to finance the program, employ the director, formulate policies for admission, interpret the work of the center, evaluate the program, and plan for the future. If the board is incorporated, it must assure that the articles of incorporation are in line with the purposes of the center. Once policies are established by the board, much of the specific responsibility of administering the program is delegated to the director.

Policies regarding admission must be in keeping with the

7. Mary D. Keyserling, "Day Care: Crisis and Challenge," *Childhood Education*, 48 (1971): 62.

stated purposes of the day care center. Policies usually determine age of admission, and specify that a child must be free from communicable disease and from mental and physical handicaps which would prevent his participation in group activities. Most day care centers give priority to the children of working mothers. Others, particularly federally subsidized programs, give priority to families receiving aid to dependent children and children of mothers who are in government sponsored training programs, such as those under the Work Incentive Program. Frequently family income is a factor in determining the eligibility of a child.

Financing is from a variety of sources. In proprietary day care centers, financing comes from the fees charged the parents. Nonprofit day care centers tend to have a sliding scale of fees, adjusted to the family's ability to pay. Such day care centers must therefore have some other sources of income. This income may come from federal subsidies, endowments, contributions, community chest or other community agencies, or from fund-raising projects. Whatever the source of funds, most centers attempt to maintain the highest quality program for the smallest possible amount of money.

Since the parents of many children enrolled in day care centers are employed, often for long hours, involvement of parents in the activities of the center must be planned accordingly. Frequently the activities of the center will be of a social nature, involving whole families rather than just parents. Parents serve on boards and committees, even though they may not be able to participate in the daytime activities of the center. Small group meetings may be planned to accommodate the schedules of different parents. Flexibility on the part of the staff is essential for the success of parent activities.

In order to ensure that day care centers will be convenient to the area where families live, facilities are often built into housing complexes. Families are not inclined to use centers which are not close by, even though the program may be superior to other services available. Locating an appropriate neighborhood space for a full day program is often difficult, as facilities such as a kitchen and rest area must be included. Also, space for a day care center can seldom be used for any other kind of activity, due to the long hours the center is in operation.

Public School Programs

Most of the children enrolled in early childhood programs provided by the public schools are in kindergartens. A few school systems have experimental programs for four-year-olds, and some have programs for disadvantaged children which enroll four-year-olds. Few nursery school programs are a part of the public school curriculums. On the whole, public school programs for five-year-olds are more formal and more academically oriented than programs for five-year-olds connected with nursery schools. This more formal structure of public school kindergartens is in keeping with the more academic orientation of elementary programs, and may also be necessitated by the large numbers of children assigned to one class.

Public schools are administered by a local school board, either elected or appointed to serve in this capacity. Policies made by the board are administered by the school superintendent and his assistants, who are responsible for various aspects of the program. The early childhood professional seldom serves in an administrative capacity except in large school systems which may employ a director or supervisor of early childhood programs. Usually the early childhood personnel who are affiliated with the public schools are kindergarten teachers.

Children are admitted to public school on the basis of age, or age plus a combination of other factors. Generally, the local school board establishes policies for admission to school, and these policies may vary somewhat from one school district to another. Usually these policies provide for enrollment on the basis of the child's reaching his fifth birthday by a specified date. (The child is assigned to a school according to his place of residence within the school district.) Some school districts allow children of above average ability to be enrolled at an earlier age. These children must be tested by the school psychologist and their ability established. They are not usually more than six months younger than the children who are regularly admitted. School enrollment is not mandatory for five-year-old children, although statistics show that where public school kindergartens are provided, almost all children enroll at age five instead of at the later mandatory age.

Financing of public schools is usually from a combination of state and local tax funds. State funds are allocated to a school district on the basis of the average daily attendance for the district. These funds are usually supplemented on a local basis to bring the support to the level which the residents are willing or able to provide. Because of the differences in the ability of different communities to provide the revenue needed for schools, wide differences exist in school funding from one state to another and from one community to another.

Parent education activities occur on a very limited basis in most public school programs. The parents of the kindergarten are usually involved in the parent organization for the total school. They may also be involved in additional parent group meetings just for parents of kindergarten children. Increasingly, public schools are planning more conferences with parents and are involving some parents in classrooms as aides. Most schools have a plan whereby some mothers agree to help the teacher with special school events.

Public schools often have very adequate physical facilities, particularly if the school is newly constructed and the kindergarten room was planned especially for children. Such classrooms often have such desirable features as toilet and hand washing facilities opening into the classroom, separate entrances for the kindergarten children, built-in lockers concealed from the classroom, and low-constructed windows. Facilities, however, may vary widely within a single school district, as some schools may be old and outdated while others may be new and modern. Many times kindergartens are housed in facilities originally built for older children, requiring that the teacher and children adjust their activities accordingly.

Laboratory Schools

Laboratory schools, usually affiliated with colleges and universities, have played an important role in furnishing programs of teacher education, child development, and family life education. Laboratory schools usually have two major goals in common: to provide a good educational program for children and to provide laboratory experiences for students. Beyond that, they differ widely in their sponsorship and programs. Some early childhood laboratory programs are part of a total elementary school; they are generally connected with a college or university school of education. Students utilize the program for observation, for practice experiences, and student teaching. Members of the faculty of the school may be considered part of the faculty of the school of education, and some may teach part-time in the school of education.

Nursery school or combination nursery school and kindergarten programs are frequently maintained as part of the child development program in either a department of home economics or family life. Such a department may also offer a curriculum in early childhood education. Often the director of the school is a member of the faculty of the sponsoring department. Advanced graduate students often serve as the teachers and assistant teachers, or a faculty member may have a part-time assignment as a teacher of a group of children and a part-time assignment as a teacher of child development or early childhood education. Children enrolled in this program will also be observed by undergraduate students who may later serve as assistants and student teachers.

Laboratory schools may also be set up in conjunction with an experimental or innovative program. The major goal of such a school is to implement the program which is being developed and to demonstrate the methods and materials which are being used. This type of school differs from other laboratory schools only to the degree that it is committed to a specific program, or is an integral part of a research program. Research is very much a part of an experimental program; laboratory schools which are a part of any well-established graduate school will also have a commitment to research.

Laboratory schools are usually operated under the administrative procedures of the college or university with which they are affiliated. The director is usually a member of the faculty, and as such has a high degree of autonomy in working with his staff, employing assistants to work on the staff, and determining curriculum. The school may operate under a budget approved by the sponsoring department, utilizing the regular college channels for expending funds. Laboratory schools are usually financed by the college or university with supplementary income from fees paid by the children who attend. Fees are not usually high in relation to the program provided. If the school is partially financed by federal funds as a part of a research or experimental project, there may be no fee at all. Enrollment is usually by application. If a new experimental program is being established, however, it may be necessary to seek the children from a particular socio-economic group. Faculty members and other people associated with the university generally want to send their children to the lab school. Assuming that enrollment is by application, they keep abreast of the situation and apply as soon as the child is old enough to be put on a waiting list. Children are admitted who meet the criteria established by the school administration, in order of the date of their application. Usually certain ages are specified, often in a given proportion if the school is small. There may be an attempt to keep a balance between girls and boys. Parents must be willing to have their children participate in research projects and must sometimes be willing to participate themselves. Usually they must supply transportation to and from school.

Parent activities depend largely on the goals of the program, and there are almost always parent meetings, conferences, and programs about child development topics. If the program is federally funded for low-income families, parent involvement may be a part of the program which is being developed and researched. There may be frequent opportunities for informal sessions for parents and teachers. Some provision may be made for students to meet with parents or to visit homes to observe the children.

Physical facilities for laboratory schools often contain special features especially suited for the program to be conducted. Very seldom are laboratory schools conducted in make-shift facilities, except for short periods of time while the program is being established. Short-term or experimental programs may be in temporary facilities, at least until the program becomes a regular part of the total college program. Laboratory schools are usually built to accommodate extra observers and participants, with large classrooms or observation booths. Small rooms for conducting research may also be a part of the facility. Classrooms for college classes may be located close by, or the laboratory school may actually be in a college classroom building. When this occurs, the school will usually have separate entrances for the children and an outdoor area separated from the campus traffic.

QUESTIONS FOR DISCUSSION

1. Compare the organization of a private nursery school with the organization of a cooperative nursery school.

2. Visit a school for young children in your town or city and evaluate it in terms of its potential for the education of young children. What would you say to a parent who inquires about it as a school in which to enroll her preschool child?

3. What standards, if any, exist in your city or state for the registration or licensing of non-public schools and day care centers? Who administers them?

4. What advantages are there for an early childhood teacher employed in each type of program discussed in this chapter?

3 | The Staff

IN ORDER TO PROVIDE A SOUND, PRODUCTIVE EARLY CHILDHOOD program, the staff must first be carefully selected and then continually offered opportunities for growth through in-service learning activities. A well-prepared staff is the prime factor in a quality program.

Staffing a school, however, presents many problems, mostly because of the shortage of qualified personnel. If current trends continue—if more children are enrolled in day care programs, if voluntary programs are provided for three and four-year-olds, and if more states fund kindergartens—the demand for teachers will continue to increase. Every kind of early childhood personnel will be needed, from administrators to classroom assistants. Specialists such as college instructors, supervisors, and school consultants will also be in greater demand.

To compensate for the shortage of classroom teachers, alternate types of personnel, such as paraprofessionals, are becoming important. Adequate training and preparation programs for paraprofessionals have still not been developed on a large-scale basis, however.

MEN AS TEACHERS

Through the years, there have been shifts in the attitudes towards men and women as teachers of children of elementary school age and younger. The "school master" of the eighteenth century was replaced by the "school marm" of the nineteenth century. Undoubtedly, one of the reasons for the traditional attitude is the belief that women understand young children better than men and therefore can teach them better. A more pragmatic reason advanced was that women can manage young children better than they can manage older, more mature pupils. Since men were believed to be needed to handle the older pupils, women moved into the lower grades and men began to dominate higher grade levels. Some school districts forbade men to teach below a certain grade level, usually the fourth grade.[1]

In recent years educators have looked more and more favorably on men as teachers of young children, largely because of changing attitudes in sex roles stereotypes. It is clear that young children, especially children from broken homes, need both masculine and feminine models to follow. School is the most obvious place to relate to male authority figures, as well as female figures. For many children the school is a woman's world. It is dominated by women's rules, standards, and activities. The same activities might be presented by a male in a manner which would give boys an idea of alternative roles they might assume.

Although a few men have found professional satisfaction in the field of early childhood education, men in large numbers are not interested in teaching nursery school and kindergarten classes. Alternative plans to regular classroom teaching might make the field more inviting to them. One program, the Indiana State University Early Childhood Assistance Program, involves men in a team approach. Under the guidelines of this plan, a male teacher who is a member of the team is committed for half a day in a given class. The other half of the day this man is on a "will call" basis and any team teacher who needs his assistance may ask for it. During the period in which he is commited to spending half a day in a classroom, he works with the same classroom for five to fifteen weeks, which gives him an opportunity to become well acquainted with the children. During the other half day he may be called on by other team teachers for specific learning activities which are masculine in nature.[2] Cooperative nursery schools have for years encouraged fathers to participate in their child's program. When men come to the nursery school, they tend to be very popular with the children.

1. Charles R. May, "Men Teachers in Early Childhood Education: Which Direction Will They Take Now?" *Contemporary Education*, 42 (1971): 222–223.
2. May, p. 224.

Courtesy of Educational Facilities Laboratories and George Zimbel

If they are comfortable in the children's activities, they often find the experience very enjoyable.

PREPARATION OF PERSONNEL

The preparation of personnel for early childhood education is a joint effort among local school systems, community groups, state agencies, and college faculties. Colleges and universities still assume a large measure of the responsibility, particularly for the preparation of leadership personnel. However, as was pointed out earlier, the current need far exceeds the capacity of these institutions. Since 1960, the number of licensed day care facilities has tripled, and the number of children in other preschool programs has doubled. The continuation of this trend would mean an increase in kindergarten and nursery school enrollment from 3.9 million children in 1968 to 6.3 million children in 1980.[3] Some steps must be taken to increase the rate at which personnel are prepared.

Two committees, the Task Force on Early Childhood Education of the Education Commission of the States and the Ad Hoc Joint Committee on the preparation of Nursery and Kindergarten Teachers, have analyzed and made recommendations for the planning of training programs for early childhood specialists.[4,5]

Their recommendations for teacher preparation include in-depth professional education in understanding children's growth patterns and learning styles, planning appropriate curriculum experiences, and dealing with children of varied socio-economic backgrounds. They also recommend programs to assist trainees in learning the human relations skills which will enable them to work effectively with other professionals and paraprofessionals. Preparation programs should be designed so that individuals may enter at the paraprofessional level and move upward to any level of professional responsibility.

Problems in the implementation of such recommendations result from the rigidity of college and university degree requirements. Also, some states have no certification requirements for early childhood specialists. Some certification programs place major emphasis on training for teaching older children, with incidental training in early education.

3. Edward Zigler, *A New Child Care Profession: The Child Development Associate*, Paper presented at Annual Meeting of the N.A.E.Y.C., Minneapolis, Minn., November 6, 1971.

4. Education Commission of the States Task Force on Early Childhood Education, *Early Childhood Development: Alternatives for Program Implementation in the States* (Denver: Education Commission of the States, 1971).

5. Martin Haberman and Blanche Persky, eds., *Preliminary Report of the AD HOC Joint Committee on the Preparation of Nursery and Kindergarten Teachers* (Washington, D.C.: National Commission on Teacher Education and Professional Standards, N.E.A., 1969), pp. 6–7.

Leadership Personnel

The leadership positions in early childhood education include college and university instructors, or any person involved in the inservice training of staff, consultants to large school districts, and state consultants in early childhood education. Leadership personnel should have broad qualifications: a master's degree or higher degrees, an ability to work with young children, an ability to relate to adults, and a familiarity with current practices, developments and research in the field of early childhood education.

Professional demands on these people are usually great, and they particularly need good health, physical stamina, emotional stability, and a willingness to go beyond the call of duty. They should also be knowledgeable in the education of children older than six years in order to relate early childhood education to the total elementary school program.

Programs for leadership personnel are usually planned carefully for each individual, including extensive work in the field of early childhood education and in-depth preparation in the supporting disciplines of psychology and learning theory, as well as leadership and research. Such training should take into account the individual's professional experiences and professional goals. Most persons who plan to accept college and university teaching positions should expect to obtain either a Doctor of Philosophy or Doctor of Education degree, although this is not absolutely essential in some college positions. Colleges and universities are being urged to be flexible about the criteria used for selecting early childhood education faculty, and are giving increasing recognition to past experiences and achievements other than the formal doctoral degree. Direct involvement in teaching preschool children is also being urged as a requirement for all college staff members involved in teacher education.

Teachers of Young Children

Most early childhood teachers should hold a bachelor's degree from a college or university, or earn an equivalent degree from an accredited four-year teacher preparation institution. Degree requirements usually include broad studies in the liberal arts as well as in early childhood education, growth and development, and learning theory, and practical teaching experiences in preschool to primary grades.

The liberal arts content encompasses the physical and biological sciences, the social sciences, and the fine arts—music, literature, and art. Professional content includes broad studies in child growth and development and teaching/learning theories, and laboratory experiences such as observation and student teaching.

Recently, colleges and universities have been moving away from the more traditional preparation program into more competency-based programs. Emphasis is placed on practical training, rather than fulfilling specific and often rigid academic requirements. Such programs are usually closely affiliated with schools and centers for young children.

Teacher preparation programs are almost always planned to meet the certification requirements of the state in which the program is located. Certification is a state function which requires that teachers meet certain specified requirements, usually involving specific courses and experiences with children. By reciprocal agreement, certification in one state may be honored by another state, but this is not always assured since requirements for certification differ from state to state. Public schools require that teachers have state certification.

Although private schools and cooperative nursery schools and kindergartens frequently have more leeway in the employment of teachers, some insist upon certified teachers as one means of assuring a quality program. These programs also may employ persons with a college degree and with considerable training and experience in early childhood education who do not meet specific certification requirements. Such teachers often have both personal and professional qualifications which enable them to be highly satisfactory teachers of young children. Most frequently these are graduates of home economics or child development curricula in colleges. Many have had extensive training in early childhood education, including background in personality development, family life, and parent education, which enable them to make a unique contribution to a school's program.

Considering the current surplus of teachers trained to teach in elementary school, it should be noted that teaching younger children requires qualifications and training different from that required for working with older children. If elementary level teachers are to be employed as kindergarten teachers, programs of retraining need to be instituted. Such programs would build on the strengths of the elementary training, but would establish the differences in educational programs for younger children. One of the crucial retraining areas is that of practical classroom experience and organization, as it is not possible to transfer the content and approach for elementary children into the kindergarten. It must be ensured that the teacher knows activities and ways of organizing classroom experiences which are appropriate for young children.

Child Development Associates

Because of the anticipated shortage of teachers in early childhood education, plans are underway for the creation by the Office of Child Development of a new middle-level professional group called Child Development Associates. This associate will have the qualifications to care independently for children but will have less academic training than those with college degrees. The associate will not replace the college trained teacher, the master teacher, or the supervisor, but will have some similar responsibilities. The associate will have achieved the minimum competencies of a good preschool teacher and will be able to plan and provide valuable experiences for children in part-time or full-day programs, or in extended day care.

The Child Development Associate certificate is unique in that it will be awarded through a national system. Training for the program encompasses many possibilities: college-based programs, supervised internship programs, and work-study programs. The credential will be awarded more on the basis of demonstrated competency rather than academic accomplishment or the acquisition of credit hours. It will give recognition to people already in the field who are qualified by experience but who may not have had formal educational opportunities. A further unique feature of the Child Development Associate program is that it is being worked out by a consortium of professional organizations concerned with the education of young children.

Paraprofessionals

Paraprofessionals include the large category of paid personnel or volunteers who assist the classroom teacher. Although they are not expected to plan and teach lessons, paraprofessionals may function in a variety of ways, from helping individual children to leading group activities. Parents are often used as paraprofessionals, as well as other people in the community who may be willing to contribute their time.

Project Head Start has been particularly successful in the use of parents as classroom aides. Some are used on a voluntary basis, but as the program has developed, policy has required the employment of aides who are parents and who come from the area served by the program. The program has been so successful that the use of parents as classroom aides has spread into the public schools.

Many school systems have found it desirable to require some basic training for aides. This training may be a two or three-week course given by the school system and conducted in a location convenient to the parent participants. Trainees are given specific information about the policies and the educational programs of the school. They are instructed in classroom routines, use of materials and supplies, and ways that they can help the classroom run more smoothly. Sections may also include discussions of the school's discipline policies and procedures.

State departments of education are being encouraged to institute a ladder type of certification which would give recognition to the levels of preparation which paraprofessionals have reached. Colleges are developing curricula in which certification could be obtained from on-the-job experience as well as previous college credit. Such programs would enable the paraprofessional to be recognized for his accomplishments at various stages along the way, and his employment opportunities would advance until he became fully qualified as a teacher.

One example of the career ladder approach is that used at Seattle's Neighborhood House Child Care Services, which has four levels. At entry, or level one, trainees observe and assume some responsibility for working with staff, parents and children. At level two, they become intern teachers and work independently. Level three is reached after the trainees have had up to three years of experience and have completed forty-two college credits. At this level, they are called assistant teachers. The fourth and final level, a head teacher, requires a minimum of two years experience and forty-five credits toward an associate of arts degree[6] which requires the completion of a two-year college curriculum.

Programs of the career ladder type may be two year programs as described above, or they may be four year programs, leading to full status as a certified teacher. Such programs may be very attractive to parents and young people who have finished high school but who did not have previous opportunities to attend college. It presents a very good opportunity for the person who needs to be working while involved in a college program.

DETERMINING STAFF NEEDS

There are many factors which help determine the staff needs of any specific program for young children. One of the foremost is the goals of the program. If the program provides day care and enrolls children from early morning until late afternoon, ample staff must be provided to allow for staggering the hours of the workers and to insure that a professional staff member will be on duty at all times. No such staggering is necessary for a two or three-hour nursery school or kindergarten. The multipurpose program also has a need for professional involvement of social workers, nurses, pediatricians, dentists, and nutritionists. Often the goals are dictated by the nature of the population served by the program. Programs serving low-income families, one-parent families, and families where the mother is employed are necessarily more comprehensive.

Physical facilities can also make a difference in staff needs. If children are housed in one large room with toilet facilities directly accessible and a direct exit to the outdoor playground, the staff requirements are minimal. If several small rooms are used simultaneously by a group of children and it is difficult to see from one part of the area to another, additional staff may be required. If the

6. Education Commission of the States Task Force on Early Childhood Education, p. 57.

toilet and playground facilities are located at a distance from the main classroom, more supervision will be needed to watch the children as they go back and forth. The age of the children makes quite a difference. The younger the children, the greater should be the proportion of adults to children. Three-year-olds need the most guidance in learning classroom procedures, such as cleaning up after classroom activities, and in learning to manage coats and boots. Five-year-olds are more independent in taking care of their own clothing, coping with minor spills, and putting away toys and other equipment. The ratio of adults to three-year-olds should be one to five or seven, with the maximum size of the group set at about fifteen children. Groups of four-year-olds should probably be no larger than eighteen to twenty, with one adult to each seven to nine children. Five-year-olds can function adequately in groups of up to twenty-five staffed by two adults. Whenever fewer adults are available, the program usually suffers and the expectation of the children usually becomes more rigid and adult-dominated than is desirable.

Extra staff are needed when exceptional children are enrolled in the program. Many schools make it a part of their policy to enroll children with handicaps, feeling that it is good for both the handicapped child and the other children to be in direct contact with each other. Children who are retarded, blind, deaf, speech-handicapped, crippled, or emotionally disturbed require extra time and attention from the teacher. If the handicapped child can be adequately provided for along with the other children, and if the teachers can be instructed in techniques which are suitable for him, a rich and satisfactory learning situation may result for all the children. Sometimes this depends on the makeup of individual class groups more than upon the staff-child ratio. It remains for the director and the board of the school to determine the ability of the school to cope with exceptional children.

Some programs have comprehensive goals and large enrollments and need elaborate administrative staff to make the program successful. Other programs are able to operate adequately with one or two staff members. There are a variety of kinds of staff that might be involved in the planning or operation of a program for young children. The staff of a large day care center might include a director, several teachers, several assistant teachers, a social worker, a nurse, a consulting physician, a consulting psychologist, a dietitian, a cook, and a custodian. In addition, there might be numerous volunteers and parents. By contrast, a small nursery school may have only a director-teacher and an assistant teacher.

School Administrator or Director

In a school with only one or two groups of children, the director may also be the head teacher, and may take care of the responsibilities of the director while teaching in the school. The director may be responsible for a program housed in one center or, as in the case of Head Start, the director may have responsibilities for several Child Development Centers. The responsibilities of the director are many and varied. The following are included:

1. Being responsible to governing board of school.
2. Selecting staff, defining staff responsibilities and supervising all staff.
3. Planning with the staff to develop school policies in relation to admission, parent activities, record keeping, and the health and safety of the children.
4. Providing leadership for curriculum planning.
5. Providing for maintenance and care of the building and grounds.
6. Interpreting the school to the community.
7. Interpreting the community to the staff.
8. Establishing and maintaining school records and reports.
9. Managing school financing.
10. Selecting, ordering and maintaining equipment and supplies.
11. Arranging for admissions to the school.
12. Providing in-service experiences for staff.

Since much of the job of the director involves working with teachers, nonprofessional staff, and parents, skill in human relations is an essential qualification. This is even more true if the school's organizational structure involves working with a board of directors. Although the board is actually the policy-making body, the director, as the professional person, is in a unique position to give leadership to the board. The director will be chosen by the board, and in matters relative to the curriculum of the school, he will have full responsibility. Part of his job will be to communicate to the board what is going on in the school and to involve them in as many ways as possible. Recommendations will be made to the board which will provide the opportunity to influence decisions which are made. Flexibility and the ability to listen to the opinions of others are important characteristics in meeting many situations. The ability to enforce policies and to maintain a working relationship with parents, teachers, and the board requires great skill.

Not all the jobs to be done around a school are very glamorous, and the director can expect for one reason or another to be involved in changing soiled clothes, washing paint off a wall, or fishing paper towels out of the toilet. Unfortunately, minor crises such as an injured child or a sick teacher do happen and the director must be able to deal with them as efficiently as possible.

Providing Staff Leadership. The director is the single most important factor in establishing the atmosphere of the school. She has to assume that every staff member wants to have a positive relationship with other staff members and with children. She also has to assume that staff members are interested in making the greatest contribution possible to the program and that they are willing to give time to experiences which will make their work more effective. She must provide the kind of atmosphere in which teachers are able to realize their potential for growth.

The director can create a situation in which freedom is facilitated and encouraged. In order to do this, she must recognize the value of uniqueness—the uniqueness of teachers, of parents, of children, of any of the individuals connected with the program. It must be assumed that each member of the staff brings to the school situation certain qualities for relating to the child, certain abilities for organizing a teaching-learning situation, and imagination. A way must be found to enhance the unique qualities of each staff member. The task, in part, is to identify the contribution each staff member can make and to provide the optimum conditions for his work. The staff member who comes to value his own experience will be more able to recognize and value the experiences of others. Directors must provide much encouragement and support, as staff struggle in the attempt to provide the best learning experience for the children.

The atmosphere of the school should reflect a mutuality—

a joint sharing between the director and the staff so that each person affects the other in the creation of the program. Creative work which is done by an individual must be appreciated by his colleagues and the director. It is the director who invites creative work, who offers support when the going is rough, and who organizes resources to provide the needed assistance.

Selection of Staff. The director is solely responsible for interviewing, employing, and dismissing staff. In actual practice, the director may seek the help of teachers in interviewing prospective staff members, particularly teachers and assistant teachers who will work directly with a new employee. Usually before a new teacher is interviewed a job description is written and a list of desirable qualifications is made to help in evaluating candidates.

Locating suitable staff often presents a problem to the director. Professional employees such as teachers, social workers, and sometimes assistant teachers can be located through the placement services of colleges and universities, through present members of the staff, or through prospective employees who contact the program seeking a position.

A local employment agency usually serves as the best source of information regarding persons for nonprofessional positions. Applicants obtained by this means must be screened carefully and, if possible, former employers contacted for references.

One of the most important factors in attracting good candidates is the reputation of the program. Prospective employees will weigh such factors as the salary, the size of the class, the location of the school, the hours the school is in session, the fringe benefits, and the possibilities for advancement. However, some of the best qualified will sometimes sacrifice other factors for the opportunity to be affiliated with an outstanding program.

The Application and Interview. The application submitted should help the director decide whether the candidate has the basic qualifications needed for the job and whether an interview to discuss the position might be fruitful.

If the candidate has a dossier filed with the placement office of the college or university he attended, these should be requested either by the candidate or the employer. Usually references included in the file will make it unnecessary to obtain further recommendations regarding the professional training of the candidate. The purpose of the application is, in part, to help the employer make preliminary decisions regarding the most promising candidates. If an interview is arranged some of the topics which should come up for discussion are as follows:

1. The school's philosophy of education.
2. The salary offered.
3. The length of the school year and opportunities for summer employment.
4. The orientation for new teachers.
5. The ages of the children to be taught.
6. Consultant or supervisory services available.
7. Evaluation of children's progress.
8. Opportunities for promotion.
9. Fringe benefits.
10. Sick leave policy.
11. Type of retirement plan.
12. Special duties or assignments.
13. Mandatory obligations to join professional organizations, if any.
14. Philosophy regarding classroom discipline.
15. Policies regarding involvement of parents.
16. Incentives to obtain further training.
17. Policy regarding tenure.

Each program will have unique features which will need to be brought out in the interview. For example, most private nursery schools and kindergartens do not offer tenure and have no retirement plans beyond social security. It is also important to note that the existence of policies may work both as an advantage and a disadvantage. If the policies are flexible and permit a staff to work together in determining how they will be implemented, they can be a great advantage. But if policies are very rigid, some teachers may find them unacceptable.

Promoting Staff Development. If professional staff are to make their best contribution, they must have opportunities for continuing growth on the job. Some of the growth experiences can be provided through staff meetings, supervisory assistance, conferences, and consultants. The job of the director must include time to plan for these. In the beginning of the year, information about the curriculum and policies of the school should be given to all new staff. The professional staff should meet regularly for planning curriculum, discussing the problems of the children both among themselves and with the parents, and planning activities for the parents.

Supervisors can sometimes help by going into the classroom and working with a teacher. Care must be taken that the teacher views this participation as help and not as criticism. A time may be selected when a special project is underway and the need for additional help is a real one.

Some directors make a practice of subscribing to several professional journals for the school, in order that recent literature may be made available to the teachers. Other directors buy new professional books and make a practice of passing them around among the staff. Teachers may obtain new ideas for use in the classroom by attending professional conferences. Often local and state professional groups hold workshops which are close enough geographically for the whole staff to attend. The director may encourage attendance by providing money in the school budget for the expenses of the trip and the conference fee. Teachers who have been stimulated by local meetings may be encouraged to attend national meetings when they are held in nearby cities.

Depending on the location of the school, many sources for consultants may be available in the local area—college and university instructors, the staff of psychological clinics, staff of hospitals, and professionals in disciplines related to early childhood education. In-service courses may be provided by colleges or universities for credit if they have ample staff to do this. Such in-service courses, if they are offered, should be based on the immediate concerns of the participants, and groups should be kept small enough to permit active participation.

There is no substitute for the interest of the director in keeping abreast of trends in child development and early childhood education. Many of the opportunities for the director to be well informed are similar to those described in the preceding section. These include reading professional journals, obtaining new books and pamphlets as they are published by professional organizations, maintaining membership in professional organizations, and attending conferences, workshops, and seminars, both local and national. Often if the director assumes some position of leadership in a professional organization, it is a stimulus to the staff.

Classroom Teachers

We are well beyond the time when it was assumed that any kindly woman or girl who loved young children could do all that is necessary for a group of children under six years old. There are personal qualities and attitudes and convictions that are necessary to the teacher's work. These characteristics do not necessarily develop during the teacher's initial teaching experiences, and they may continue to develop for as long as she teaches.

The teacher has the major responsibility for planning the experiences that her pupils will have. She needs to have had sufficient experience as an assistant or intern to feel secure in making decisions about curriculum and to feel comfortable in leading a team which may involve assistant teachers, interns, volunteers, or parents. She should be able to organize her classroom activities to utilize the abilities of the team, guiding them in their work with young children.

A very crucial part of the teacher's role is understanding the attitudes and values of the culture and adapting her style of teaching to the different students involved. The teacher should be familiar with the methods that are effective with different socio-economic groups, from poor children to middle-class children. The teacher creates the classroom ambiance which promotes good learning. It is her responsibility to observe and understand the individual needs of each child and to plan a program which will enable each child to have the maximum growth experiences.

In recent years an effort has been made by teacher educators to define the competencies that a teacher of young children will need to develop. These competencies will provide a basis by which persons long-involved in teaching young children can be recognized for the abilities they have developed through experience rather than through formal training. They also provide a basis upon which more effective teacher education can be planned.

Haberman and Persky[7] have suggested the following list of competencies as a basis for evaluating teacher performance or planning experiences for preservice teachers.

1. *Foster independence*—arrange materials so they are accessible to children, give assistance but do not intervene unnecessarily in situations children can handle themselves, select and use equipment children can operate themselves, arrange furniture and materials so children can work independently.
2. *Encourage a positive self-image*—take time to listen to children, respond to children's questions, give praise freely when appropriate, receive parents warmly.
3. *Provide intellectual stimulation*—use daily-life experiences and materials to develop concepts, introduce a wide variety of learning resources, ask thought-provoking questions, respond knowledgeably to children's questions.
4. *Promote creativity*—provide materials and encourage individualistic use of them, accept and appreciate divergent responses, create interest in imaginative stories, use music, dance and other arts to encourage individual responses.
5. *Encourage socialization*—provide activities that stimulate interaction of children with each other and with adults, find ways to involve isolates, help children discover ways of interacting without resorting to aggression.
6. *Promote physical development*—provide food and rest as needed, include both quiet and vigorous activities in the program, use outdoor facilities when feasible, secure medical examinations and treatment when needed.
7. *Contribute to emotional development*—comfort children who are upset, model a healthy emotional response, deal with conflict without being judgmental, vary expectations for children on the basis of knowledge of tensions in their out-of-school situations.

7. Haberman and Persky, pp. 8–11.

8. *Collaborate and cooperate with other staff*—identify appropriate responsibilities for individual staff members, show willingness to delegate or assume responsibility, set appropriate goals, assess progress toward goals.

The Social Worker

A social worker is recommended for the staff of Head Start, a day care center, or any early childhood program having a number of families that can use the assistance. The social worker is employed by the school just as any other member of the staff is. She should be a graduate of an accredited school of social work and should have had some experience in working with young children and their parents.

The social worker should be responsible for making the study of the family prior to the child's admission to the center. She may be very helpful to the family in deciding whether or not to enroll the child. Usually the social worker is the first person on the staff to meet parent and child and to observe the parent-child relationship. The intake study should consist of several interviews with the parents during which the social worker obtains information about the family situation and the developmental history of the child. Parents should be informed of such factors as hours, fees, school policies, admission procedures, and possible reactions of the child. The social worker can also inform the family of other community resources and services so that they can evaluate the best way to meet their needs. She may also counsel parents on personal problems affecting the child-parent relationship.

The social worker's ability to work with the staff is crucial to her success and to the success of the program. By sharing information about the family and the child and by helping the teacher interpret the child's behavior in terms of this information, the social worker can do much to enhance the teacher's ability to plan for and guide the children. Her contacts with parents do not take the place of those between parents and teacher, nor of contacts that parents have from time to time with the health staff or with the director. The social worker is a member of the staff team and must have full knowledge and appreciation of each staff member's contribution.

Health and Nutrition Personnel

Health care for the children is primarily the responsibility of parents, yet it is the responsibility of the school or center to see that steps are taken to insure the health of the children. Every program needs to have a physician available for consultation. Health care for children in day care and Head Start programs especially should be under the supervision of a qualified physician.

Preferably, the physician serving a day care center should be a pediatrician and should have some training or background in public health. Ideally, the physician will be involved in planning and carrying out the total day care program. He should be available to staff and parents for consultation on health problems and for emergencies. He may give direct services if indicated by the particular situation.

If a nurse is employed by the school, she is usually available for a portion of the day. She inspects children as they arrive, talks with parents about the health of the children, and administers first aid when necessary. Occasionally, she conducts individual and group conferences with parents. She sets up and supervises the record keeping procedures on the physical condition of the children. A school can often obtain the services of a nurse on a part-time basis. It is desirable for a nurse serving in this capacity to have some public health training.

If meals are served, consultation should be available from a qualified nutritionist regarding the planning and preparation of well-balanced meals. The nutritionist should have a college degree with a major in dietetics and, if possible, some special work in child feeding. She should plan the meals and supervise the food preparation. Where a nutritionist is not available, some assistance may be obtained through a local school lunch program or from a home economics teacher.

The Assistant Teacher

The assistant teacher is referred to in various ways—as a teacher's aide or paraprofessional. The responsibilities of these people vary according to their abilities and experience. It is important to the program that the assistant teacher be able to assume the responsibility of the teacher if necessary. She should assist the teacher throughout the day in the care and education of the children. To the children she should be as important as the head teacher. Some may even relate more closely to the assistant teacher than they do to the head teacher. She must represent to the child the same authority, love, and protection that the head teacher does. In emergencies she should be able to take sole responsibility for the group.

Since the responsibility for planning rests with the head teacher, the assistant teacher should accept the teaching philosophy of the head teacher and learn to work with her as a team mate. The assistant teacher should be informed about each child and his family so that contacts with children and parents reflect a consistent approach. If she gains information about children, it should be shared with the teacher. Assistant teachers should attend staff meetings, attend parents' meetings, and assist in the care of the classroom and supplies.

Additional Staff

The size of the school has a great deal to do with the size of the supporting staff. Secretaries and bookkeepers will be needed according to the number and kinds of records kept. Teachers, directors, social workers and health staff all keep records on children's progress, and if these are to become a part of the permanent file, they must eventually be typed and filed.

Some programs will engage paraprofessionals as social worker aides and parent education aides. Volunteers may frequently contribute several hours a week to perform such duties as assisting the teacher with special activities, giving special attention to a child, using special talents in art or music, or accompanying classes on field trips. They can also be very helpful when a regular teacher is absent. Volunteers can also assist in the office, repair toys, act as babysitters while mothers go to group meetings, and escort children to and from school.

Kitchen and maintenance staff perform the very important roles of preparing food and keeping the premises clean and sanitary. The people who serve in these positions must have the same liking for children as those more directly involved with them, because their relationships with the children play an important part in the education of the children. Usually it is also necessary to have the heavy cleaning done at a time when the children are not present. The janitors or custodial staff who do this may be a part of the school staff, or they may be a part of the larger maintenance staff of the building.

A good staff is one of the most important factors in a quality program for children. Each person must be qualified for his job and feel a sense of responsibility towards it and the children. Not only must the staff be qualified, they must get along well with each other. Good relationships among the staff help to provide models of the behavior children should learn.

QUESTIONS FOR DISCUSSION

1. Assume that you are the director of a cooperative nursery school that enrolls sixty children in the morning and an equal number of children in the afternoon. About two-thirds of the children are four-year-olds. The remainder are three-year-olds. Plan the staffing needs of the program.

2. Assume that the program described above is a day care center. How would the staffing needs differ from the cooperative nursery school?

3. Plan an interview that you would hold with a prospective teacher for the cooperative nursery school described in question one.

4. Plan an interview that you would hold with a prospective cook for a Child Development Center. How would it differ from an interview you might have with a prospective teacher?

5. Plan and role-play a staff meeting involving the director, teachers, and assistant teachers of a school, focusing on the topic "How can we help the children be more creative?"

4 | Facilities For Early Childhood Programs

THE CHILD RESPONDS TO HIS ENVIRONMENT FAR MORE ENERgetically and immediately than does an adult. The child is in the process of discovering space, distance, levels, heights, and how he fits into these new dimensions. To him a little bit of height is a hillside from which he can survey the world, and a covered space beneath a table is a secure hideout. He needs space where he can explore freely, yet he also needs a spot where he can go when he wishes to be alone for awhile.[1] A setting should be simple so that a new child can find his way about, yet varied so that children do not become bored by its obviousness. Space is the heart of a good living-learning environment and must be organized to accommodate the learning activities in a functional manner. The organization of space and the placement of centers of interest dictate the flow of learning activities.

Both the site and the space, as well as the furniture and equipment, must be adaptable, to permit activities to expand, shrink, or move outdoors. Portable furniture and movable carts, cabinets and screens can all be made part of a modifiable setting that takes on new dimensions as new demands are met. Learning tools must also be displayed and accessible for use. A stimulating environment can be achieved only when children are able to reach objects of choice and spontaneously begin their activities. The environment should encourage independence. This includes a functional world at the child's level. Clothes lockers, drinking fountains, furniture,

1. Ronald W. Haase, *Designing the Child Development Center* (Washington, D.C.: Office of Child Development, 1969) p. 13.

windows, sinks, toilets, mirrors, tables, storage units, clocks and door knobs, should be tailored for a child's use. Allowing the children to be independent requires an environment designed with adequate safety precautions: shatterproof glass in windows and doors, rounded corners on furniture, shock-proof electric plugs, slip-proof rugs and floors, and regulated hot water temperatures. Items such as light switches, doorknobs to unsafe areas, sharp scissors, and medical supplies should be out of a child's reach.

PROSPECTING FOR SPACE

When prospecting for space, several things should be taken into account. If a building is being sought for a given community or neighborhood, the location of the facility is the primary consideration. If no convenient facility can be found, there probably will be no school. Parents either do not want, or are not able, to take little children long distances. If a seemingly suitable facility is located, the building should be inspected by health and safety authorities to determine exactly what renovations must be made to make it sanitary and safe. Without this inspection much money could be spent making the building attractive only to find that it will not pass inspection and cannot be used as a licensed facility. Another very important factor is the adaptability of the building to the program. Often it is possible to adapt the program to the building. But it is necessary that the building can really serve the program.

Old Schools

Occasionally schools which are structurally sound have been abandoned for public school use because they are no longer large enough to serve the area population and because space will not permit an addition. If the school has been constructed within the last fifty years, the possibility of remodeling may be feasible. A building older than that would probably be very costly to modernize. The educational program should be defined and the architect should determine whether the structure can be adapted. A piecemeal job is not recommended. It may seem inexpensive at the time, but it will probably prove more costly over the years.

Family Houses

Some people feel that it is easier to achieve a home-like atmosphere in a house than in any other type of facility. Frequently houses do have features which make them particularly appealing, such as bay windows, open living room ells, carpeted floors, and sheltered driveways. In selecting a house for this purpose one must consider such things as division of space, location, exits and fire escapes, the toilet facilities, and the heating system. It may not matter that the house is divided into small rooms if walls are removable or if small rooms are needed for the program. The outside doors on houses do not ordinarily open outward as is required for a school. Frequently there is only one exit from the basement level and from the second floor, which will not satisfy state safety regulations. Since newer homes may have more than one bathroom, remodeling them may be relatively easy, but older homes with one small bathroom on each floor will present problems. Heating systems for homes are not usually enclosed in fire retardant structures, as is required for schools.

Storefronts

The use of a storefront is one of the least satisfactory arrangements for adapting space because the building is located right on the street. Such a facility may not offer space which can be used for a playground. The greatest asset of a storefront is usually a large space unbroken by walls. As in an old house, some of the disadvantages are likely to be inadequate toilets, an unsafe heating system, little storage, and poor lighting and ventilation.

Educational Facilities of Churches

Many churches have facilities designed specifically for a weekday school. Rooms in churches built years ago may be quite small and toilet facilities may not be readily available for use by the children. Since churches increasingly see the operation of a weekday school as an appropriate community service, they make their facilities more and more satisfactory and available. As a public building, the church may already meet certain health and safety requirements. The major disadvantage in the use of church facilities is the sharing of classrooms by two groups of children. Usually the bulletin boards must be cleared off on Friday afternoon and some of the supplies must be put away. Before school on Monday they must be put back in place. If the church has planned well, however, there should be ample storage for the weekday and Sunday school. Once the routine is established, the inconvenience need not be too great. Since much equipment is shared, there are advantages to both programs.

Prefabricated Classrooms and Mobile Homes

The use of prefabricated buildings and large trailers has become a way to supplement existing building space. It is a way that schools can provide for increased enrollment in an area, without expensive permanent construction. When no longer needed in one place, such buildings can be moved to other locations. The portable classroom can be designed specifically with its purpose in mind. Units can be grouped in different ways, and some units can be used for offices and research space. These are especially adaptable to experimental programs and to those areas which have land but no usable existing facilities.

LOCATION OF FACILITIES

The childhood education program should be directly related to the community. This can best be accomplished when the school is near the families that it serves. In areas where most families have private cars, close proximity may not be quite as essential. However, in areas where parents depend on public transportation, or where public transportation is expensive or inconvenient, the school must be accessible. Ideally, the school should be within walking distance of the children's homes, along safe streets.

Increasingly, preschool classes are visited by high school and college students preparing for parenthood or other responsibilities of citizenship. Students preparing for vocations such as teaching, pediatrics, nursing, social work, and the ministry also greatly benefit from experiences with young children. Because of the tight schedules of these students, location will be a factor in determining their use of facilities.

The site selection must take into account the zoning laws, which frequently require that schools be located in areas zoned for business, taking them away from the residential area much preferred for young children. The features of buildings located in the area under consideration will also influence the kind of structure suitable for use. It is desirable, if possible, to select a site which will not be in an area of heavy traffic because of the danger to the children.

DESIGNING NEW SPACE

Defining the steps leading to the creation of the best possible environment for young children is much easier than accomplishing them. Haase[2] has indicated the process that might be followed:

1. Develop a precise statement of the school's goals. State clearly and specifically the philosophy of the program as developed jointly by the staff and the parents.
2. Establish the program based on the goals. Particular attention must be given to the roles of different individuals in the program. This is comparatively simple when the staff consists largely of two or three teachers. But when parent volunteers, pediatricians, and social workers, as well as nonprofessional staff are involved, the individual must understand how his role supports the roles of others.
3. Describe the nature of the environment needed to house the program. Visualize the most effective use of spaces, equipment and furnishings. Engage the services of an architect who knows how to use space and materials at minimal cost to achieve desired results.

The architect, staff and parents should continue to work together for some time after the school has opened. It takes time for the staff to learn to make the best use of the facilities and for

2. Haase (1969), p. 20.

problems to become evident. Some physical changes may need to be made to meet new needs as they appear.

INDOOR SPACE

The School Entrance

The approach and entrance to the school should be designed so that it tells the child that school is a nice place to be. Its exterior view should be warm and inviting.

Once the child becomes familiar with the school, the parent may leave him at a drop-off point where he can proceed to enter alone. The child should be able to enter the building unassisted. Once he can do this, he feels much more independent than if the parent goes all the way into the classroom.

The mother who drives her child to school will need a place to park while she watches him go into the building. If the children arrive by bus or in car pools, the driver will need a place to park without blocking the way for other cars and other children. A covered canopy which takes an indirect route from the drop-off area to the doorway can allow this even on a rainy or snowy day.

Whether the child goes into an entrance hall or directly into the classroom, the first area that the child sees should be attractive. Pictures, perhaps pictures which are changed regularly, or decorative objects will help make the entrance area more interesting. This is also a good place to put the parents' bulletin board.

Administration

The director requires a quiet office area in which to meet with parents, visitors, and staff. The administrative area could be one office in a small school, or it could be a separate area broken into a reception area, offices, and meeting rooms. If the school is very small, such an area may not be economically feasible, although some inconvenience will result to both the staff and those who come to the school.

The children's records and school administrative records will usually be kept in the school office. If there is sufficient space, each teacher may be able to have a desk in the office. If not, space for a teacher's desk may be provided in the classroom. Cabinets for holding children's records can also be recessed into the classroom walls. Additional offices will be needed for such members of the staff as the social worker, psychologist, or dietitian, if these professionals are employed by the school.

Kitchen help, housekeepers, and janitors need storage facilities for their work materials and personal belongings. Any participants or observers need places to leave coats, books, and other materials. The presence or lack of space for these activities will affect the program to the extent that these groups of people are constantly involved. When many people are involved and no space is provided for them, it may cause undue disruption for the teachers.

Conference Room and Staff/Parent Lounge

The need for a conference room or lounge depends on the size of a school and the size of the staff. The major function of such a room is to give teachers a place to get away from the children for a while, to smoke, drink coffee, chat or take a nap. Here a teacher or parent may relax and chat with another teacher or parent. Parents may gather informally for discussions, or they may drop in on their way to observe the children. The conference room may also be used for a parent class while the children are in school, or it may be used for staff planning meetings after the children have gone home. Opinions differ as to whether there should be separate rooms for staff and for parents. If both are possible, they should be in close proximity. Possibly a movable partition should separate the two so that a larger room would be available for shared activities. In any case, the decor should be bright and friendly. This room might be equipped with a one-way vision screen into a classroom, permitting the observation of children. If a one-way screen is provided, it should be possible to close it with drapery in order to keep activities in the two rooms entirely separate at times.

Observation Areas

Some schools are built with the specific goal of allowing students and other visitors to observe child behavior in a preschool environment. Teachers are often able to improve their methods as a result of observing other teachers in action. One often overlooked group of potential observers is the children themselves. Though sometimes the observation area has been considered off-bounds to the children, they may be able to learn as a result of watching other children engage in activities.

There are arguments for and against the use of an observation room. Those who do not like observation rooms feel that they are often not able to see all parts of the room in which the children are engaged in activity. They also feel it is difficult to understand conversation unless the children are on the near side of the room.

Some consider the use of an observation room an invasion of the children's privacy. Such arguments, however, are answered by pointing out that the observation room is not intended for spying and that concealment is probably a negative value. Some argue that one-way vision helps to protect the privacy of the children by preventing direct exposure to so many people. The parent who sees his child through a one-way vision screen will believe what he actually sees. Many times there is no other way to convince a parent that his child behaves as he does.

Observation areas are provided in a number of ways. The most common is a one-way vision screen or glass which permits those in the room to look out while those on the other side of the glass or screen cannot see in. Such an arrangement usually requires amplification of sound through the use of microphones scattered throughout the area occupied by the children. The room should be large enough to hold a counter or desk for observers to use for note-taking. There must be room enough for persons to pass in and out behind observers without disturbing them. Observers should also be able to enter the room without disturbing the children's activities.

Another type of observation space is a balcony overlooking the classroom area. One particular advantage of this type of observation area is that it does not take up valuable wall space. Replacing the observation room with technological equipment is also being tried in some facilities. One advantage is that a television tape allows children and teachers to view themselves. A distinct disadvantage is the limited range of the camera and the dependence of the observer on the operator of the camera for selection of what is to be observed.

Toilet Areas

The first consideration for the children's toilet area is that it be accessible from all play areas in the school. Whether there is a single toilet area or several toilet areas depends on the number of children enrolled and the utilization of the indoor space. Recommendations for the number of toilets range from one fixture for each five children to one fixture for each fifteen children. As a rule of thumb, it is probably wise to provide one fixture for each eight to ten children, but never to have fewer than two fixtures. When the number of children begins to approach forty or fifty, it is wise to create several dispersed toilet areas. This assumes that children have considerable freedom to move around and that toileting is geared to the child's need and is not a group-directed activity. The main toilet area or one of the dispersed areas should be directly available to the outdoor play area so that it can be used as easily as possible. This will also enable the teacher to keep an eye on the child without actually having to accompany him inside.

Special adaptations in the toilet area should be provided, according to the age and abilities of the children. The recommended height for toilets for children three through five years of age is eleven inches.[4] These are the typical junior fixtures available from most plumbing manufacturers. If younger children are to be enrolled, still smaller fixtures will be needed. A cleanout should be provided to allow retrieval of flushed toys, paper towels, and other objects that children may throw into the toilet and which block the drain line. The floor of the toilet should be of liquid plastic, ceramic tiles, or sheet vinyl. It should be seamless, to promote a minimum retention of water and odor. Concrete does not make a satisfactory floor as urine will get into hairline cracks and produce odors. Toilet paper, paper towels, soap dispensers, mirrors and lavatories should also be at child height. The child should be able to manage the faucets of a low lavatory himself, and a low platform should be added if the lavatory is too high.

Separation of toilet rooms for boys and girls is very much a culturally determined issue. Depending on the social orientation of the community, some parents may prefer separate facilities. With

4. Fred Linn Osmon, *Patterns for Designing Children's Centers* (New York: Educational Facilities Laboratories, 1971), p. 57.

young children, however, the widespread practice of having the children all use one toilet area is believed to encourage a healthy attitude toward sexual development. From the teacher's point of view, the lack of separation, or separation by low partitions, is helpful in allowing her to supervise the area and give children the needed assistance.

Usually the toilet rooms are quite open, with low partitions between the toilets and without doors. Doors in particular present a problem if they have locks on the inside, as children may lock themselves inside. Doors also contribute to bumped heads and mashed fingers.

The installation of a bathtub should be carefully considered for an all-day program. A bathtub would not be used daily but when children stay at school all day they sometimes need an all-over bath before they go home, particularly on hot days when they have been playing outside.

Quiet Area

Teachers find it very convenient if the school has a small room which can be used for quiet activities. This might be a room where a teacher can take three or four children for a story when other activities are so noisy as to prevent enjoyment of the story. It might be the place where two or three children can rest quietly and look at books. Here also children might work puzzles or have a special science experience. It isn't so much what particular activities take place in the room, but rather that there is a quiet place where a few children can get away from the rest of the group. In buildings which do not have a room specifically for the purpose, teachers can devise all kinds of ways to create a quiet place. They use a section of a conference room, sometimes part of an office, or they may be able to use the end of a hall.

If possible, the floor should be carpeted or covered with a large rug so that children can sit on the floor or use the floor as their play area. Comfortable chairs, colorful cushions, and pictures on the walls add to the room's attractiveness. Children should be helped to understand that the room is for special activities, and children who want to run or play vigorously should do so in another place where vigorous play is acceptable.

Storage

Storage space should evolve from a general building plan that in turn reflects the theoretical premises of the program. If the teacher is to be efficient, materials must be made accessible to the children without requiring constant teacher attention. Materials used daily should be stored in a convenient place. Other materials, such as musical instruments, science materials, and picture files, need not be stored in the immediate area where they will be used. Some equipment, like snow shovels, sleds, and wading pools, are seasonal and can be put in more remote storage when out of season to make room for materials which are needed immediately. Consumable supplies for snacks and lunch may need special refrigeration or storage. Every school has auxiliary equipment which presents a real storage problem because of its bulk—such as corn poppers, cooking equipment, animal cages, and fish tanks.

Storage for all these items will not be concentrated in one spot. Some materials will have to be accessible to all teachers. This seems to necessitate some kind of central storage area, as well as storage located near specific areas such as the entrance, kitchen, clinic, classrooms, and conference room.

The garment storage should be placed near the entry to the classroom to minimize the amount of water and snow that is brought across the floor by the children's shoes and coats. This area should be easy to maintain and should not become slippery when a good bit of snow or mud has been tracked in.

Although lockers should be located near the entry, location in the entry is usually unwise. If the lockers are in the entryway, on rainy days it can become too congested. With children and adults struggling to put on boots, coats, and sweaters, parents and other children will find it virtually impossible to get in or out without stepping on someone. Since the child may also need to put on his wraps before he goes out to play, the lockers should be accessible from the outdoor playground without having to go through the classroom.

Supervising of this area is very important. The area should be visible from at least part of the classroom. Teachers usually need to give some help to the children, especially the nursery school children. Children sometimes like to put things in their lockers or take things from their lockers during the day; so for convenience there should be no need for additional supervision when they do this.

Teachers do not agree on the best location of lockers. Many teachers do not like them in the classroom because they are unsightly. Keeping coats hung up and materials from falling out is almost impossible. If storage is located against the wall, it takes up a lot of wall space that might have a better use. If it stands free in a part of the room, it takes up a great deal of floor space. A separate room offers the advantage of having the mess of snow and water out of the classroom.

Storage units can be of several types, depending partly on personal preference and partly on space available. Many teachers prefer the open locker with one or more shelves at the top, hooks for clothes, and space below for boots. Doors are considered a hazard and are not usually provided. There also are portable trolley type units with hangers for coats, but teachers usually prefer not to use these because preschool children find it difficult to manage the hangers and the coats. If the program lasts all day, space will need to be provided for blankets, pillows, and linen. A larger tray or drawer or a separate storage unit is usually needed for this purpose.

Children's lockers are usually marked with their names to help give a sense of possession. Sometimes they are also marked with pictures of animals or with other types of decals. The use of names seems far more important than other types of symbols, as it helps to establish the child's sense of identity. He knows it is his name even though he is unable to read it. Photographs, if available, may make an interesting variation for a child who has never had very much to call his own.

The Clinic

A room is needed in the school for children who become ill or who may be coming down with a communicable illness. If the mother is at home and can come for the child, the child can remain in the clinic or isolation room only until the mother comes. If the mother is working, the child may remain in the room for a longer time.

The program that houses the slightly sick or convalescing child in the isolation room for longer periods of time will need to provide more than the usual cot in an otherwise almost empty room.

It would be desirable for this to be a homelike bedroom with a rug, table and chairs, and toys for the child's use. The room might be an extension of the play group environment where the child is temporarily detained but not really isolated. If the center is large enough to have a nurse on duty, the isolation room may be partitioned off from the nurse's office or a larger health room.

Kitchen

The need for a kitchen varies greatly from one program to another, depending on the number of hours the program is in session and the meals which are served. Schools which prepare and serve hot breakfast and lunch for their children need a complete kitchen, with plans and procedures approved by the local health authority. This kitchen should be separate from the group play environment but adjacent to the area where the food is to be served. Where practicable, it is desirable to have a "pass through" from the kitchen to the room where the food is served. If the "pass through" is low enough, children will be able to help with the serving. If there is no "pass through," food can be placed on tea carts and wheeled to the room where the children are to be served. Giving children an opportunity to put their dirty dishes on the cart and take back a dessert affords a great deal of satisfaction and tends to encourage eating the food which is served.

In centers not serving complete meals, kitchen facilities need not be extensive. For snack preparation there is a need for one or two heating elements, refrigeration, a sink with hot and cold water, work counter space, and storage for food and other supplies. The area should have containers for trash storage and be well ventilated. These same facilities may be used for food preparation which is conducted as part of the educational program, if designed for both teacher and child use. Kitchenette facilities will also be useful for serving light refreshments at parent meetings and other social events which may be a part of the school's program.

Classroom Area

The classroom area may consist of a single self-contained area or a series of rooms for a group of children. Much depends on

Courtesy of Educational Facilities Laboratories and George Zimbel

the size of the total facility, as small schools cannot be expected to provide a separate room for different activities. The space shared by several groups of children may actually be quite open. Such arrangements may also enable the creation of privacy in some areas.

The children's classroom should be a friendly, pleasant place which the child can readily recognize as his. The furniture, equipment, and practically everything in it should be scaled to the size of the child. Pictures, bulletin boards, and other display materials should be hung at the child's eye level. Some of the windows should be low enough so that he can see out.

Spaciousness is one of the most important characteristics of the classroom. Authorities differ on the exact amount of space which should be allowed for each child. Usually from thirty-five to sixty square feet per child is available. A classroom with only thirty-five square feet per child may be acceptable if there is additional space in the building where the children can go for active play. For the majority of classrooms, forty to fifty square feet per child seems desirable, recognizing that if the room is used for lunch and afternoon naps as well as morning activities the maximum space will be needed to allow transition to take place smoothly.

For children's rooms good light without brightness is required. Experts generally agree that direct sunlight should rarely be allowed to come into the room, and windows in the sidewalls should be properly glazed or shielded to control brightness.[5] Electric lights should be as unobtrusive as possible. This can be accomplished in part by having as little contrast in brightness as possible between ceiling and light source. Areas of either high or low brightness can cause fatigue and loss of visual accuracy. It is recommended that specialists be consulted regarding ways to provide a satisfactory lighting system.

5. Foster K. Sampson, *Contrast Rendition in School Lighting* (New York: Educational Facilities Laboratories, 1970), p. 91.

Courtesy of Educational Laboratories Facilities and George Zimbel

Colors used in the room do much to determine lighting effectiveness. A white or off-white ceiling with walls and other large areas of light shades of color are important reflectance factors. Light-colored floors are also important for lighting purposes and are easier to keep looking clean than are dark floors. Light colors on the walls also provide a pleasing background for children's paintings which might be displayed. Unfortunately, light-colored walls show paint spots and hand prints, so that it is very important that the finish can be easily cleaned.

Areas around sinks should be protected with a vinyl or washable formica surface. Nursery school and kindergarten walls need much display space, situated low enough for the children to see and mount their own work. A small blackboard for the children to write or draw on is a nice addition to a nursery school or kindergarten classroom.

With loud activities in the classroom, such as block building, carpentry, housekeeping play, and music, the noise level can be somewhat controlled by paying attention to acoustics. Wall and ceiling construction can be designed for sound absorption. Sound from floor surfaces is appreciably reduced if carpeting is used on a major portion of the room. Draperies also help to absorb sound and often are placed in classrooms as much for this purpose as for attractiveness.

With children spending time sitting on the floor, floor surfacing is very important. Such factors as resilience, comfort, maintenance, durability, and acoustical control should be considered. Carpets are increasingly installed in classrooms, covering at least a portion of the floor. For areas that need frequent cleaning, linoleum, vinyl, or asphalt tile are recommended. Maintenance of wood floors is a problem. Bare concrete and terrazzo floors are durable but their hardness and coldness make them less satisfactory. Whatever the floor surface, regular maintenance is a must. The amount of time which children spend working and playing on the floor makes its cleanliness an important sanitation factor.

Centers of Interest. The classroom should be arranged into centers of interest to provide for different activities. The major centers needed are:

Block Area. Usually two kinds of blocks are recommended: the large hollow blocks with which children can build large structures, and the smaller floor blocks with which they can make roads, bridges, railroad tracks, and castles. Included in this area are the small accessory toys that are to be used with the blocks, such as small cars, buses, airplanes, and tractors.

Housekeeping Area. This area contains child-scaled equipment such as a stove, sink, cabinet, table and chairs, doll bed, carriage, and other kinds of accessories such as dishes and brooms that go along with keeping house. Equipment such as the doll bed and the doll carriage will be most satisfactory if they are large enough to hold a child.

Library Area. A quiet corner should be provided where children can look at books. Books on topics related to the interests of the children should be attractively displayed. A small table with chairs, and perhaps some small rockers, make the area inviting.

Music Area. The piano and music-listening area should be positioned so it does not interfere with other activities. Listening is greatly facilitated if there are earphones so that the music does not raise the noise level of the room. There should be an open area near the piano so that children may gather around for singing.

Art Area. Easels need to be placed so that both water for washing and racks for drying can be easily reached. If there are no easels, tables can easily be set up for painting. Children can also use the floor, after covering it with newspapers for protection. Tables that are large enough to hold large pieces of fingerpaint paper and clay boards should be set up near the storage receptacles for crayons, paste, clay and other art materials. Usually these are in the same general area as the easels, in order that all the art activities may be supervised by one teacher.

Carpentry Area. The area for construction is the noisiest of all areas. It is ideal to have a separate woodworking room or a porch where the workbench can be moved when weather permits. In addition to the workbench, equipment usually consists of saws, hammers, clamps, nails, and soft wood. The tools should be real but small in size. Different-sized pieces of soft wood should be provided for hammering and sawing.

Science Area. A table or the top of a low cabinet should be provided for science displays, science materials, and experiments which are in progress. Continuing projects like an aquarium or a terrarium may be a part of this area. This may also be the area in which the teacher places new and interesting objects with science learning possibilities. Much of the science equipment, such as cages, magnets, magnifying glasses and pulleys, may be kept in the teacher's storage.

Math Area. As children reach kindergarten age the teacher should begin to include material in the classroom for the development of simple mathematical concepts. Materials might include the larger concept blocks which are designed to teach colors and shapes, dominoes, number puzzles, a play clock, and sets of numerals. These may be in a separate area, or they may be in the area with other quiet materials.

Quiet Area. All classrooms need some place where children are able to sit quietly and work a puzzle, put pegs in a board, or work with simple put-together table toys. For older children, lotto games, matching games, and counting games are usually used in this area, although they may not always be on the shelf for the children to use at any time they choose.

Criteria for Choosing Equipment

Some equipment and materials will need to be selected with the social and cultural interests of the community in mind. In some areas, locally manufactured products, cultural trends, or religious customs should be remembered in selecting equipment. For example, some schools may wish to have both light-skinned and dark-skinned dolls in the housekeeping corner.

Certain factors are important to consider in purchasing equipment for a nursery school or kindergarten.

Safety. Everything possible must be done to see that equipment is safe. Construction of equipment should be carefully examined. There should be no sharp edges; paint should be non-poisonous. Toys such as guns and pistols are not usually considered appropriate school equipment, because they present real safety hazards when pointed directly at someone's face, the way most children use them.

Sturdiness. The constant and continued use of scohol equipment makes durability a prime prerequisite. Equipment must be of the best construction in order to avoid high repair and replace-

Courtesy of Educational Facilities Laboratories and George Zimbel

ment costs, and most of all to avoid accidents. Good equipment may cost more initially, but it is worth the investment if it lasts twice as long and needs little repair. Ability to withstand harsh weather conditions may be a factor in choosing equipment which is permanently installed outdoors. Strength may also be a factor with equipment which older children use. Any equipment which is not given some measure of protection must have unusual strength and durability to withstand weather and use hazards.

Interest Level. To be worthwhile to children, equipment must stimulate interest. Interest is related to the variety of ways the child can use the toy and to its suitability to the child's individual skills.

Such characteristics as curiosity, initiative, resourcefulness, imagination, and creativity are influenced by the toys and materials children are given to work with—such as blocks, play people, dolls, wooden or plastic animals—and the guidance given in the use of these toys. Some of the most stimulating materials are those which are simple and useable in a variety of ways by children of different

Courtesy of Educational Facilities Laboratories and Rondal Partridge

ages. Raw materials such as sand, water, clay, and paint have endless possibilities. The youngest children enjoy the sensory experience of feeling and manipulating the materials. Ideas and feelings can find expression through their use, as children become familiar with the possibilities of the medium.

Encouragement of Large and Small Muscle Activity. Young children are learning to climb, to ride wheel toys, to lift, to pull and to push. Equipment which helps them to do these things will assist in the development of large muscles essential to coordination and movement. It is also important that they have activities which help in the development of smaller muscles and in eye-hand coordination such as working puzzles, building with small blocks and other construction toys, and handling art materials.

Encouragement of Social Learning. Some materials promote growth towards independence, exploration, and social relationships. Equipment such as blocks and housekeeping materials encourage children to engage in dramatic play in which they imitate the roles that they have observed adults engaged in. This requires that they play cooperatively with other children. Through this dramatization, they are able to learn much about the responses of other children and to understand some of the puzzling bits of information which have come to them through their daily experiences.

Acquisition of Cognitive Skills. Some toys should be selected because they specifically stimulate language development, create an interest in learning to read and identify letters and numbers, and encourage the use of various cognitive skills such as classification and concept development. Books, large letters, large numerals, matching games, and counting games definitely fall in this category.

CRITERIA FOR SPACE AND EQUIPMENT

Some space is definitely more difficult to arrange. Some rooms do not have electrical outlets where they would be most convenient. The physical characteristics of the room, such as the heating system, are often important factors in determining where specific pieces of equipment should be placed. Sometimes it simply is not possible to put every piece of equipment in the kind of area that should contain it. Some rooms will need to be changed several times before a satisfactory arrangement is worked out. Some of the principles which seem helpful are given below. Some of the principles have been referred to in the section on areas of interest but they will be repeated here for easy reference.[6]

1. The classroom should be arranged to provide centers of interest. From time to time, some of these centers of interest will be replaced by other centers of interest, but basic centers such as the block building area and the housekeeping area should be in the classroom continuously.
2. Popular centers of interest should be widely separated to distribute children throughout the room. Implementing this principle will sometimes be difficult, but it is very important in terms of the atmosphere of the classroom and the number of conflicts the children have.
3. Objects often used together should be placed close together. This prevents a lot of needless running back and forth across the room. It is also suggestive to the children. This does not mean that children should be limited to using the equipment only in the area of the room in which it is placed. Some children have very creative ideas about the uses of equipment, and the teacher should encourage them to express these ideas.
4. Messy activities should be placed near washing facilities for ease in cleaning up. Art activities in particular should be placed near the sink if possible. Children with paint on their hands tend to get the paint on everything between them and the sink. The temptation to stop and play with something else before cleaning the paint off is too great to resist. Clay, water, play dough and messy play materials should also be fairly near the sink.
5. Every classroom needs to have available some open space where the children can construct large block buildings

6. Bureau of Child Development and Parent Education, *Equipment for Children in Kindergarten* (Albany: New York State Education Department, 1960), p. 48.

and where there is enough space to move around smoothly. Usually, a large space is also needed for story time. One single open space is usually enough, since the activities for which it is needed are not carried on at the same time.

6. Art and block-building activities should be placed away from avenues of traffic. Screens or shelving can be used to divert traffic around these activities. If children walk freely through areas where others are building with blocks, the temptation to knock over a building is almost too great to resist, and fights are apt to result. Walking through the art area results in paint not only on hands but also on clothing.
7. A slight separation of the housekeeping area is conducive to dramatic play. In more conventional classrooms, shelving or low screens can create this partition. Some housekeeping areas are raised above the floor level to form a balcony which is accessible by steps. Some rooms have natural alcoves in which the housekeeping area can be tucked away. The separation which is provided should allow the teacher sufficient view for supervision without interfering with the activities of the children.
8. Quiet activities should be grouped away from avenues of traffic. Placement of tables or storage cabinets is usually sufficient to divert children around the quiet activities. If there is a carpeted area, the quiet activities may be placed there so children may play on the floor. Grouping activities in this way can help children learn to respect the rights of other children not to be disturbed. If children are continuously disturbed, they tend to leave and engage half-heartedly in something else.
9. The arrangement should encourage children to be independent in using and putting away materials. Items should be placed on tables or shelves where it is easy for the children to get them out and put them away. Storage cabinets with doors are discouraging to children when it comes to putting things away. Children tend to throw materials into bins so that materials there are always disorganized. Materials should always be stored in the

same place. If the child knows where specific materials go, he can return them more easily.

HOUSEKEEPING

Keeping the room neat is greatly facilitated by ample storage shelves for the materials that children use and places for materials that have been temporarily put away.

The mess created by many desirable curriculum experiences presents an almost insurmountable problem for many teachers. Painting, working with clay, and some of the other most worthwhile activities for children make the biggest mess. Generally, the more freely the teacher can permit the children to use the materials, the more worthwhile their experience. Yet the teacher may be under tremendous pressure to keep the floor clean. Newspapers and large plastic dropcloths can protect a carpet and can measurably cut down on the clean-up job. The teacher should try to strike a happy medium in insisting on neatness without interfering with the child's freedom of activity.

There should be places to store paintings, clay, and woodworking projects. It is interesting to observers and parents to see these materials out because it shows the kind of work the children do. These products need to be worked into the general scheme of the arrangement so they don't just look like clutter. Nothing is more helpful in dealing with this problem than having enough space.

Custodial staff need to be helped in understanding young children so they do not constantly wage war with the teacher over the mess. Just as real carelessness on the part of the teacher should be avoided, so should a curriculum which is controlled by the custodian. A regular cleaning schedule should include a clean-up by a group of children after every use of the room, with weekly cleaning of floors and other heavy cleaning tasks.

OUTDOOR SPACE

The outdoors provides many opportunities to stimulate the child's learning. Some of the experiences which feed a child's curiosity are very simple, such as watching the patterns clouds make in the sky, feeling the wind, discovering tadpoles and birds' nests, and walking on one's shadow. When young children are brought together in groups, adequate outdoor play space is essential. There should also be opportunities for exploring, discovering, and learning on the playground and the other grounds that surround the school. Many activities can be carried on much more easily outside than inside. We need to think of the outdoors as being as important as the indoor areas.

Landscaping

For children who live in crowded urban areas, outdoor landscaping and play areas are particularly important. Shrubs and flowers of various sizes and colors can be a continuous source of pleasure and add a new sphere for observation. Low shrubs provide places for exploring and hiding. Trees may not only provide shade, but may also provide leaves and seeds that children can use in multiple ways.

Garden Plots

If the outdoor area is large enough, the children can have their own garden plot. Ideally, each child should have his own individual plot that he can plant and tend. Short of that, a single plot could be planted by the group. Usually, quick growing plants such as radishes and lettuce are quite satisfactory. Zinnias and petunias make satisfactory flowers as they withstand hot dry weather and a good deal of neglect, while providing many flowers to be picked. Garden plots should have full sun and adequate water sources. Growing things that can be brought inside when winter comes continues to afford the children the opportunity to water the plants and watch them grow.

Playground

The outdoor playground is best located where it will have some protected sunny areas in the winter and some shaded areas in summer if possible. Location on the south side of the building is particularly desirable in the winter in cooler climates. Large open

Courtesy of Educational Facilities Laboratories and George Zimbel

areas should be provided for running and riding wheel toys. Secluded areas are nice for individual play when children do not wish to be disturbed by their more active classmates. A semi-sheltered area often makes this section of the playground usable in weather which might be too wet to permit the use of the entire playground.

Estimates of the amount of space needed for the outdoor

playground vary from 100 to 300 square feet per child, with 150 square feet per child about average. Maximum use of the playground requires that all surfaces be well drained to encourage fast drying, including the grass and dirt areas. Every playground should have more than one type of surfacing. If possible, there should be grass, so that all children can experience the delight of playing on and with the grass. The grassy area usually has to be located away from the building in order to permit it an opportunity to grow. There should be some hard surfacing, probably of asphalt, concrete, brick, or stone, near the entrance to the classroom. One section of the playground should include some tanbark or sawdust to provide a softer surface for climbing. The constructiveness of play is often improved if part of the hard-surfaced area takes the form of a walk or roadway where children can use tricycles, wagons, and doll carriages. Curves in the walk also help to prevent spills which may occur if children have to make abrupt turns on a squared-off corner.

A large sand area encourages children to play together, carrying out projects like building mountains or roadways. A large wooden or concrete enclosure is necessary to keep the sand inside. Raised areas or boards that the children can sit on and use for pushing trucks loaded with sand are useful. Not so much is spilled if these boards are inside the sandbox rather than around the edge.

The value of the playground will be severely limited unless outdoor storage is provided for all movable equipment. Everything that is not anchored in concrete must be locked inside a storage shed each evening. This also prevents weather damage to the equipment. Sometimes the storage shed can serve a dual role as a play house, with some equipment from the inside brought out on a daily basis. Putting equipment away at the end of the day is a job that the children can learn to do themselves.

Safety is an important consideration in planning the playground. An enclosed playground relieves the teacher of an area of heavy responsibility, as there is almost always some child who will run out of bounds. Many people object to the high prison-like fences that enclose some schools. Such a fence might be necessary to prevent vandalism, but no such fence is needed for the children. An attractive yard-type fence is all that is needed if the children understand that its main function is to keep them safe. There will be little problem with the children climbing it as long as there are other things to climb. Often part of the fence can be shielded by the use of shrubbery so that it does not detract from the beauty of the grounds.

The location of the playground in relation to the street is another factor in safety. Traffic is the greatest hazard for young children. Parents who drive their children to school should be able to drive onto the grounds to prevent the child from having to go near the street.

Choices should be available to the child: not only what to play but whether to play. A child should be able to decide whether to play alone, with a small group of children, or with a large group. Each of these activities requires a distinct kind of space: small, sheltered areas for solitary play, more ample places for small groups, and an open space for group activity.

Recent years have seen the rise in popularity of playground equipment in the form of sculptured animals of concrete, metal, or vandal-proof plastic. These are usually attractive to the adult, but after an initial spurt of interest from children they tend to go unused. Children need much simpler things, such as mounds of dirt, empty boxes, or the trunk of a tree. The more simple the object, the more it encourages the children to play imaginatively. A cardboard box can be almost anything to children—a boat, a car, a house, or a rocket ship.

Many activities carried on in the classroom can go on outside. Music belongs outside as much as inside; although teachers seldom think of it, instruments or drums can be used outside with great abandon. Dramatic play has many possibilities, and a few properties, such as a doll carriage and doll, may be almost enough equipment. Books and stories belong wherever children are—under a big tree or around a table made of a cable spool. Often the materials of science and mathematics are more at home outside than in the classroom. The child raises a car on the climber with the pulley or measures the road constructed in the sand. Many animals can be better provided for outside when the weather is warm than in the classroom. The far end of the playground can be used for picnics.

Indoor and outdoor space can both be used to advantage when it is possible for children to move freely from one area to the other. Although it is expected that each child will spend a part of each day in each area, children will gain from following their own individual patterns of play if there are rich experiences both inside and outside.

QUESTIONS FOR DISCUSSION

1. Select a nursery school or kindergarten classroom that you know and redesign it to make it as convenient and attractive as possible. This should include all changes in the physical aspects of the building, including relocation of plumbing and entrances if necessary.

2. Design the facilities for a new laboratory nursery school for approximately thirty-five children, to be constructed on a portion of the first floor of a new child development building.

3. Visit a kindergarten classroom in a newly constructed elementary school and make a drawing of the floor plan and the outdoor area. Make a list of the equipment that you would recommend for purchase for the classroom. Show how you would arrange the furniture and equipment in the room.

4. Redesign the outdoor area for the kindergarten room described above, including the equipment you would purchase and how you would arrange it to make the playground as inviting and educationally stimulating as you think it should be.

5 | Admission and Grouping Policies

A PROGRAM WHICH IS GOOD FOR SOME CHILDREN MAY NOT BE good for others; therefore, the policies which are set up to determine who is accepted in the program should help to fit the right child to the program. These policies may also be helpful to a parent who is looking for specific types of experiences for the child or for himself. For example, one parent may want a school which expects participation of parents; another parent may not want to participate and may seek a school which has more incidental involvement from parents. Admission policies can be a very important factor in determining whether the parent is pleased with the program of the school.

A clear statement of policies is particularly important in any program which has more applications for enrollment than it can possibly accept. Parents who have been turned down go away more satisfied if they know on what basis the decision was made.

ADMISSION POLICIES

Admission policies are of vital importance to parents because they determine whether their child is eligible to enter a program. Many parents like to know that the choice is open to them to enroll a child in an educational program, although they may not actually take advantage of the opportunity. With children under the age of six or seven, school attendance is not usually compulsory, and parents have a degree of choice. Social pressure would certainly be strong to place the five- to seven-year-old child in school, but pressure might be equally strong to have the younger child remain at home.

Teachers are equally concerned about admission policies because they help to determine the potential enrollment in their classrooms. Teachers with strong preferences for how and what they will teach may also have strong preferences regarding the enrollment of children who can best profit from their instruction. Teachers are often able to exert strong influence in the development of enrollment policies.

Guides for Developing Admission Policies

Although the absence of publicly supported educational programs for young children is considered a disadvantage, this may be an advantage when the survival of a program depends on its ability to meet and satisfy needs as the parents and community see them. Hopefully, some of the inferior programs will not last and the more effective programs will continue. Divergent programs mean a greater likelihood that the needs of many parents and children can be supplied.

Purposes of the Sponsoring Agency. Sponsors of an early childhood program often have specific reasons for sponsoring it. If the purpose is to serve as many children of a community as possible, regardless of race, color or religion, admission will be open to anyone who wishes to enroll. In other words, if a child is of the specified age, a parent only needs to submit an application or follow another outlined procedure to enroll the child. This has the disadvantage of creating a situation in which minimum control is exercised over the number of children admitted. Other programs serve more specifically defined groups. The enrollment policies of the Head Start program are, in part, established by the legislation which specifies that funds allocated for the program must be used for children who come from low-income families. Some day care programs may be open only to the children of working mothers.

A specified type of school population may also be affected by admissions policies. For example, the Nurseries in Cross-Cultural Education represented a deliberate attempt to plan to involve families from Oriental, Caucasian and black racial backgrounds, and from middle and lower income groups.[1] One of the stated

1. Mary B. Lane et al., *Nurseries in Cross-Cultural Education* (San Francisco: San Francisco State College, 1971).

purposes of this project was to encourage greater community participation by these groups in a rapidly changing area of San Francisco. Although this purpose was accomplished, most programs do not have such ambitious objectives. They may nevertheless have purposes which make them unique. A cooperative nursery school would probably have a policy that makes admission contingent on the willingness of parents to be involved.

Ages of the Children to be Enrolled. Every program has some specifications about the age of children to be enrolled. The large majority of publicly supported programs set a specific date by which the child must reach a specified age in order to be eligible for enrollment. A few programs have a more flexible policy which permits younger children to enroll as long as they demonstrate certain intellectual abilities. Private institutions are often more flexible with regard to the age of children enrolled. In the interest of good public relations between public schools and other educational programs, however, the smaller programs are almost forced to conform to admission age requirements close to the public school admission age.

The Needs of Parents in the Community. Where programs are not publicly supported, they tend to develop out of the needs of people in the community. Cooperative nursery schools develop in communities in which there are young, middle-class parents in two-parent families in which the mother is not employed. Day care centers are more likely to be organized in communities in which there is a need for supplemental care for the children of working mothers. The program, as well as the admission policies, will probably be affected by these factors.

Number of Children. Often the number of children is limited by the space available to the program. The intent of such a policy is to set the enrollment at the number of children which the program can adequately serve. Overcrowding reduces the quality of the program, and admission policies can help prevent this.

Enrollment of Exceptional Children. Many schools have policies which provide for the acceptance of exceptional children, not only because they feel they can provide a good experience for the exceptional child, but also because they feel that the exceptional child provides a good experience for a normal child. For any school which wishes to include exceptional children, a permissive policy statement may be developed which will enable those responsible for enrollment to consider any child who applies. Consideration can then be given to specific problems. Will special demands be made on the teacher? How many other children are already in the group and what kind of special attention do they require? Will this child require an undue amount of the teacher's time? Is the teacher qualified both personally and professionally to develop the program required by this particular child? Are the necessary materials and facilities available to provide for the maximum development of the child? If, after thorough consideration, accepting the child seems desirable, specific steps for admission can be worked out with the parents.

Children who are extremely aggressive or hyperactive create special problems that require professional expertise. Any classroom which already has problems of this sort among several of its children probably should not take more children who will also need this kind of additional attention from the teacher. Too large a proportion of children who require special attention can be a deterrent to a good program.

The greatest need of the exceptional child is to be treated like other children. The exceptional child must also learn how to give and take, how to follow rules, and how to share. The exceptional child may provoke the sympathy of adults and may have unusual difficulty in being allowed to develop the independence that is especially important for him. A school setting provides the child with contact with adults who are less emotionally attached and who may therefore offer a growth experience that he may never have at home. Whether the child is blind, deaf, crippled, mentally handicapped, or gifted, he needs to play with normal children, insofar as he is able.

In the interest of both the normal children and the exceptional children, the school must maintain the right to make an individual decision about each child and the group in which he is placed. A group which might not be able to take a blind child might be able to accept a physically handicapped child. The proportion of exceptional children to a group must always be small, perhaps one or at most two, even in classrooms providing the optimum staff and physical facilities. Teachers should be supplied with as much information as possible about the child and should receive assistance from trained personnel in understanding the specific needs of the child. They should work closely with the parents in planning programs and activities and in discussing problems which arise.

FACTORS AFFECTING ADMISSION

The most important factor in deciding whether to admit a child to school is the individual child's emotional readiness to be separated from his mother. This follows closely in importance after the factor of the mother's readiness to share the care and education of her child with other adults. Unlike entrance into public kindergarten, the child's entrance into a nursery school is usually based on many family-related circumstances. Each family has its own basis for making decisions, and places different values on the types of experiences they can provide for their children. A family that values intellectual experiences, and lives in a neighborhood where there are many other such families, may find nursery schools readily available and widely accepted. A rural area may not commonly have wide attendance of children in nursery school programs, and parents in such areas may be less eager to send their children. In order to provide a child with a program in rural areas, parents might have to take him a distance of several miles each day and call for him at the end of the program. Many mothers might feel they could not afford the time and expense.

Sometimes other children in the family make a difference in the decision. If the mother has several preschool children, she may feel they derive a great deal of benefit from being together. Some mothers try to teach their children to function independently and to feel comfortable with other adults and children, while some mothers are emotionally dependent on their children. The former would probably enroll her child, while the latter would avoid enrolling him or might remove him from school after he had been enrolled. Parents should be encouraged to think through factors such as these before enrolling the child in school. It may be better for the child to remain at home a year longer while both child and mother develop further readiness. No mother should be made to feel guilty because she decides to keep her child at home another year, but she should be helped in providing a good experience for him while he is at home.

Teachers are usually aware when parents send their children to early childhood programs simply to avoid having them at home. Such attitudes are revealed by things parents do and say, and often these children are better off in a good program where they can be accepted and helped to grow in ways their home does not afford.

Age of Readiness

A child must have reached a given age before he will be considered for most schools. The age which is set may more often relate to the purposes of the program, the space, and the staff than to a specific child's ability to profit from a program. Most nursery schools which are not limited to a small group of children begin admitting children when they are three years old. In this sense, the term three years old is often very widely interpreted and means more specifically two years before the child is eligible to enter public kindergarten or three years before he is able to enter first grade. There is nothing magic about the age of three. Some children may not be ready to leave their mothers at this age, and others are ready some time prior to the age of three. The age of three years is selected because it is about the time that children begin to enjoy playmates and show a social interest in other children. Also at this time they are beginning to enjoy group activities, such as listening to a story for a short time. Curiosity is quite high at age three, and the large majority of children respond favorably to many new activities.

Practically all four-year-old children can benefit from a school experience. Often parents who feel they can afford to provide only one year of school experience wait until the child is four to enroll him. Some states are instituting publicly supported programs for four-year-olds, feeling that valuable time for intellectual learning is lost if programs are not provided by this age. Usually when a child as old as four does not respond well to a program, it is due to factors other than age, and some evaluation must be made to determine whether the program selected is appropriate for the child.

Kindergarten or other programs for five-year-olds have long been accepted by many communities, and although kindergarten attendance is not usually compulsory, almost 100 percent of children are enrolled. Acceptance is less general in communities where kindergarten has not been provided, and many parents may feel that children are too young to go to kindergarten. Facts do not support this. Most five-year-olds are ready for a school experience, but the experience provided for them may not be appropriate. This is a curriculum problem and should not be confused with the ability of a five-year-old child to be stimulated by a good educational program. Overcrowded classrooms and curriculums too structured for five-year-olds create an unfavorable situation for both the teacher and child.

Some nursery schools require that children be toilet trained before they are admitted to school. Some parents feel that toilet training should be complete before the child moves into the wider environment offered by the school. Most nursery school teachers expect to guide the development of children in managing themselves. Toilet accidents are a common occurrence even among children who supposedly are toilet trained, and the nursery school teacher will not be upset by them. Toilet accidents may also occur in kindergarten, especially at the beginning of the year.

The child's ability to participate in the program without physical or psychological damage is important both for the child's own protection and the protection of the other children. This and other health policies will be discussed in a later chapter.

When the influence of the various factors is considered, how the child's family feels towards having him in school is probably the decisive factor in determining whether he goes or not. Remembering this, the preschool teacher should help each parent understand what the school has to offer the child and what responsibilities it places on the parent.

Some people have expressed the opinion that early childhood programs will replace the family as the strongest influence on children. Early childhood professionals have always viewed early childhood education as a means of supplementing the home and in no way as an influence undermining the influence of the home. Parents who feel their influence is weakened by having a child enrolled in a specific program should seriously consider whether they wish to enroll the child at all. The fact remains that no school experience is truly satisfactory unless both parents and children are happy with it.

Planning with the Family for Admission

The ease with which the child makes the transition from home to school is often dependent on the preparation of his family and the school. In some families the child's experience will have served to prepare him; in other families the transition needs to be planned. A child who has had varied experiences with other people and who has happily been away from his mother for short periods of time usually expresses little unhappiness when left at school. A child whose experiences outside the home have been very limited and who is very dependent on his mother may be reluctant to have her leave him at school. Occasionally, however, the child who would be expected to look forward to school does not. He may go for a few days and then decide he does not want to go. This behavior is perplexing to both parent and teacher and neither may be able to discover the reason for it.

Preparing the child should begin some time before school actually starts. Planning in the spring with parents of children who will be admitted the following fall is an important step. Suggestions can be made to parents in a group meeting, in an individual conference, or by means of an introductory letter.

Prior to school entry all children should have had some experiences playing with other children, including playing with other children in their homes. For many children these experiences happen naturally, but for only children who live where there are few, if any, other children of their age this will need to be planned. The school may be able to help by suggesting another child who will be entering at the same time that the child may visit. The lack of such social experiences may be the reason why a parent seeks preschool experience for his child, yet the change should be gradual enough to give the child a chance to grow and develop a readiness for the school experience.

Once it has been decided that the child is going to school, several more direct steps can be taken. The child can be invited to visit the school. At this time the child can see children doing things he would like to do, and he can actually participate if he feels like it. The mother can also show the child how he will enter and leave the school. All of this should be done very casually, the purpose being to give the child an idea of what to expect and not to sell it to him.

Several kinds of visits are successful in helping children become familiar with the school. Some schools encourage visiting in the spring before the child starts school, to enable the child to see the physical setting and to observe what other children are doing. This should be a short visit of not more than an hour, at a time of day when the child will enjoy the activities.

Another kind of visiting simply involves the physical setting and the teacher. The parent brings the child to the classroom for a short time to show him the room and some of the materials that he will be using. The child should be given time for some exploration to find the equipment and materials which interest him. The teacher uses this time to talk with the mother and to get to know the child.

Sometimes two or three children are included in these visits, but the number should be kept small and the visit informal. Sometimes this initial visit takes the form of an open house and involves not only the child but also both his parents, as well as his brothers and sisters. Brothers and sisters who are just one or two years older than the child often can be instrumental in promoting his interest in school. Most younger children should probably stay home at this time, as they may require the attention that rightfully belongs to the child who is being enrolled. At other times it is appropriate for a younger child to come to the school with a parent, but parents should not usually be permitted to leave younger children at school to visit. Sometimes younger children can be invited, but the time for this should be determined by the school.

If visiting is not possible, the teacher might indicate to parents some of the materials or activities that will be available for the children during the first days of school, so the parent can familiarize the child with some of the things he will find there. Parents should be careful not to give school such a build-up that the child is disappointed. Also, parents can be helped to be aware that remarks made by older children about school may make a deep impression on a younger child, especially the teasing remarks about how he will be treated and what he will not be allowed to do. Parents are not always above using the fact that a child is going to school to get him to do things he otherwise refuses to do, making him feel like a baby if he doesn't do them. Going to school and the child's feelings about it are so important that nothing should be allowed to spoil his positive feelings about it.

If the child is entering kindergarten, teachers may have expectations of things the child will be able to do, such as managing his own clothes, including his coat and boots, and tying his own shoes. Not all five-year-olds can do these things, but they will know more about doing them if someone takes the time and patience to help them. Children this age also take pride in being able to tell people their names and addresses. This is important for them to know when they have their first opportunities to go places on their own. Children of this age are also interested in their telephone numbers and may be able to remember them.

Adjustment difficulties may occur even when all the right things have been done. Children may react by doing unpredictable things. Some well-prepared children may cry, while other less-prepared children do not cry at all. Some of them start to suck their thumbs when this habit seemed to have been discarded. Some of them wet the bed when this has not occurred for several years. Some become irritable and bossy and generally difficult to live with. These are quite normal reactions and do not persist very long. The teacher can often help the parent acquire a more objective attitude toward the situation when there is really little cause for alarm, or can assist in acquiring help if it seems to be needed.

Planning First Days at School

Each child takes a step towards maturity as he becomes a participant in a nursery school or kindergarten program. Part of the responsibility of the school is to help the child make the transition to school in a way that helps him and his family to appreciate this growth. The child needs to feel that he has entered a whole new enchanted world in which both the activities and the people are a source of pleasure and learning. The parents need to take pride in their progress in releasing the child to the school group and in his ability to become a part of it.

The younger the age at which a child is enrolled in school,

the more his parents will be involved in the process. The teacher will need to explain the enrollment process so that the parent knows what to expect. This explanation should include such things as whether the mother is expected to remain at school with the child on the first day, how long she is to stay, how the mother can help the child during the visit to the school, and some behavior to expect during the adjustment process. Parents of three-year-olds are well-advised to plan on being accessible during the first few days in case they are needed. Four and five-year-old children usually move into the school experience with only one or two days introduction. No child should be left by his parent until he indicates an interest in what is going on and seems to want to participate, even though it means that a parent may need to sit in the room for several days. The school maintains the leadership role in determining such policies and should not permit a parent to drop off a child on the first day for a full session without any prior orientation or any arrangement for how she can be reached.

Orientation of Parents. Parents need to be given information about the program of the school and about specific requirements that are made of them. Usually this information can be provided in a group meeting and is of vital importance to parents and teachers in schools which do not conduct initial interviews with parents. Cooperative nursery schools will need to hold much more extensive orientation meetings prior to the beginning of school, as will any other program where extensive participation by the parents is expected.

Interviews. Providing an initial conference with every parent helps to build good relationships. Most parents have questions about the program, and this provides an ideal time to answer them. It also helps the teacher gain general infomation about a child. This initial contact provides a good basis for future conferences between teachers and parents. An individual conference is more desirable than a group meeting where there is little room for interaction.

The First Day at School. Simplicity is usually the rule of the first day. Keeping the group small and keeping the time shorter than the usual school day are two practices that usually should be followed. This assures that the teacher will have enough time to give attention to each child and that the children will not become over-tired. Usually in kindergarten it is not necessary to plan short sessions for more than one or two days. Special arrangements can then be made for children who need more time to adjust. In nursery school, especially with three-year-olds, much of the first week may be used for orientation. If most of the children seem ready for a full session, there seems little justification for keeping the session short. Once the children are identified who need more time to adjust, special arrangements can be worked out with their parents. These parents will often need reassurance that the behavior of their children is entirely normal.

Teachers should be expected to help the parent and the child by identifying the expected behavior. Teachers may make such statements as, "Your mother will sit over here where you can see her while you drink juice with the other children," or, "Your mother will help you hang up your coat and then she will say goodbye to you," or, "You have had a very busy day; tomorrow you will be able to stay by yourself." Parents usually expect such direction by the teacher and respond well to it if the teacher is clear about what she expects.

A few tears may be inevitable, even with the best of planning. A child who has been happily engaged in activities with his mother present is not likely to cry very long when she first leaves. Mothers should never be permitted to slip off from their children. The consequence of such behavior is often that a child clings to her the next day, refusing to let her leave. The child should be treated with the respect that would be shown to any other person. He should be told by his mother that she is leaving and that she will return at whatever time has been designated. When the mother does return, the teacher can reinforce the behavior by saying, "Mother said she would return after we finished our playtime and here she is now." The mother can feel needed and appreciated, yet the child can be allowed to develop the necessary independence.

Sometimes children also cry when they don't want to go home. The teacher can help by statements such as, "All the children are going home now. Mother will bring you back tomorrow; then you can have another turn on the climber." The teacher must show appropriate understanding of the child's feelings but must be firm about the fact that school is over for the day. Most children accept the routine after the first day.

One of the common plans schools follow for groups that have children of more than one age is to have all the children who were enrolled the year before come on the first day. This will give them a chance to renew their friendships and to become acquainted with new teachers if there are any. It also gives parents an opportunity to talk together and with the teachers. These children very easily move into the routine of the day and usually function independently from the very beginning. New children can be added two or three at a time on subsequent days, first coming for about an hour and staying longer as they seem ready for it.

Another satisfactory plan is to divide the children into two groups and have half of them come the first hour and the other half come the last hour of the session for one or maybe two days, depending on whether it is nursery school or kindergarten and whether the children have been to school before. This has the effect of both shortening the length of time and reducing the size of the group. On the second and third days the teacher might have half the children for the full session, with all the children coming for the full session on the fourth day. In kindergarten classes where it is sometimes difficult to arrange a staggered enrollment, the teacher may be able to arrange to have half the children come the first day and half the second day, with all of the class coming for the first time on the third day. If the teacher should not happen to have an aide or a student teacher to help her during those first days, a parent from the previous kindergarten group could provide assistance.

Activities planned for the first day should be relatively simple. The room should be set up so that it is attractive and so that materials will interest the children. At this time there should be some materials which the children already know and which can be used with relatively little assistance from the teacher. Children should have an opportunity to use the materials accessible in the room before they are expected to sit still for a discussion or a story. Group activities should be kept very short.

Transitions from one activity to the next are difficult, especially with the youngest children. The more gradually they can be done, the more the teacher can permit individual children time to finish what they have started. As the children become more familiar with the routine, transitions will become easier and smoother, although there will always be some children who have problems.

AGE OF ENTRANCE TO PUBLIC SCHOOL

The age at which children should start school has been a hotly debated issue for many years. Perhaps this is why many states have settled on the age of seven as the time when school is compulsory. It becomes accepted to go to school at whatever age the public school permits children to enroll. For over half the children in this country, this means near their fifth birthday, when they have the opportunity to attend kindergarten. According to a recent survey,[2] in 1969 there were no states with compulsory kindergarten and compulsory attendance. Effective in 1973, seven states have statutes for compulsory provision of kindergarten and optional attendance. This means that each school district affected is required to provide a public kindergarten. Forty-three states or territories have permissive kindergarten statutes. These statutes allow the school districts to provide public kindergartens, but only thirty-seven provide state aid for the support of the kindergartens.

Since 1965, when Head Start was initiated under the Economic Opportunity Act and Title I of Public Law 89-12—the Elementary Secondary Education Act—made public kindergartens possible for low-income children in some states without kindergartens, another trend has been noticeable. Top priority in the area of early childhood education is being given to children from depressed areas, as programs are available to them which are not provided for other children. It seems to be well established that these children have the greatest need for the experience. There is evidence of support for programs for all children in the number of states that have pending legislation that would provide public kindergartens.

Evidence indicates that children as young as three years can find value in a school experience; therefore to debate whether children should be admitted to kindergarten at age four and one-half

2. Battelle Memorial Institute, *Final Report on Preschool Education* to Ohio Department of Education (Columbus, Ohio: Battelle Memorial Institute, 1969), p. 75.

years or at five years becomes quite ridiculous. There are educational programs which are appropriate for children who are four years old just as there are programs which are appropriate for children who are five years old. The question of the age of entrance can only be answered by considering it in relation to the kind of program to be provided. Unfortunately, the practice of making programs for kindergarten and primary children oriented more toward the early teaching of academic skills has also served to push the age of entrance upwards. As kindergarten teachers are more and more under pressure to include the teaching of academic skills in kindergarten, they become increasingly aware that many of the children are not ready for this kind of program. They are sensitive to the needs of the children and to the abilities which they exhibit. Rather than subject children to programs which are inappropriate for them, they have often insisted that children should be older when they enter kindergarten. There is absolutely no justification for raising the age at which children go to school because the curriculum is too hard for them. It should be the school's responsibility to adjust the curriculum to the child. This is what education is all about. We have seen the effects of inappropriate curriculum experiences on children from depressed areas. We must accept the importance of matching the educational experiences to the readiness of the child. Experiences so planned tend to be attractive and interesting, and yet challenging enough to encourage learning. This process of teaching and learning is as applicable to the four-year-old as it is to the six-year-old, although the content may be different.

Nevertheless the age-of-enrollment controversy persists. One school system says a child should be five by September 15, and the adjoining system says a child should be five by October 1, and yet another district says the child must be five by January 1. If a family moves from one locality to another, a child who was in school for the fall may not be eligible to continue in the new district. The problems are many and are not easy to resolve. No one convinces parents whose child has already been in school for one or more years that their near five-year-old is too young to go to school. The main advantage for using age as the criterion for school entrance, from an administrative point of view, is that it is specific and eliminates making decisions about the child's readiness. This policy is easily administered, understood by all, and supposedly treats all fairly. It gives no recognition to the developmental abilities of the child or the wishes of the parents.

EARLY ADMISSION

Because of the differences in the developmental level of five-year-old children, some school systems have instituted plans of early admission. Under such a plan criteria are established which are thought to be indicative of advanced development, and a testing program is instituted. Children who satisfy these criteria are eligible to be enrolled before they reach the age required by the usual enrollment policy. The child may be as much as six months younger than the usual age of admission, but usually no more than that. The general reaction of parents to this plan is more favorable than to a specific age-of-entrance policy. The plan is generally not well liked by teachers, many of whom feel that while younger children often have the intellectual abilities to succeed in the program, they sometimes do not have the same social abilities and physical control as the other children. Sometimes parents hesitate to enter their young children because they are aware of the feelings of teachers and fear that these feelings might influence the teacher's reaction to their child.

Opinion remains strictly divided regarding the merits of such a plan. Some schools have been using a plan of early admission for years with apparent satisfaction. The children who are admitted early are reported to do as well as the other children. It is felt that the program is an effective means of recognizing some of the individual differences of the children. On the other hand, other schools have instituted a plan of early admission only to abandon it after a few years. Reasons given for this are that test results made at various stages in the child's school years show that the children who are admitted early do not do as well in school as older children of equal intellectual ability.

Testing programs of the type required are expensive to administer, and if all children are to have equal opportunity for testing, they should be made available to the parents at no cost by the school system. If a charge is made, such a program is discriminatory because not all parents can afford to have their children take the tests. One of the most important reasons for abandoning this testing program is the effect it is believed to have on children. The prestige factor connected with early school entrance by children is very important to parents in some communities. These parents sometimes put a great deal of pressure on the psychologists to make sure that their children are eligible for admission. Sometimes this pressure is so great that children considered ineligible for admission experience the feeling of school failure even before they are admitted. Despite the promise of early entrance plans, it may be well to consider whether children should be subjected to this kind of pressure.

Clearly, the issue of early entrance is not easily resolved. Where there is flexibility and willingness to adjust to individual children, the child who has advanced abilities should do quite well. Where the curriculum is fixed and children must do a great deal of adjusting to it, the older child will have a distinct advantage. In fact, when older children in a class are compared to younger children in the same class, the advantage is in their favor. It is better to be the oldest and the brightest, rather than the youngest, though bright. Many parents are well advised to enroll a child in nursery school rather than in kindergarten if there is any doubt of his readiness for the experience.

Children are seldom bored in a quality kindergarten program, but parental pressure for academic achievement often means that children are placed in programs that have little meaning for them. The school is charged with the responsibility for providing the right experiences. Whether they are able to do this often depends on staff and facilities. The teacher of an overly large class without the aid of an assistant is in no position to provide the kind of program needed by any child who must have a large amount of individual attention. It is usually unwise to enroll an under-age child in this type of classroom.

GROUPING POLICIES

The basic consideration in deciding how to organize children into groups of class size is how best to meet their individual needs for education and development. In any situation in which children are placed in groups, the individual child must make some modification of his behavior to conform to the expectations of the group. With very young children, the ability to do this is extremely limited. Groups are usually kept small and activities are kept flexible to enable the children to be as natural as possible.

Age Groups

The criterion used for assigning children to groups has traditionally been age. Four-year-olds are grouped together, three-year-olds are grouped together, and five-year-olds are grouped together. Sometimes the groups represent even smaller distinctions in age than one year. Such designations as younger fours and older fours are quite common where the school enrollment includes more than one class of children of the same age. Grouping policies are easy to formulate when age grouping is used. As long as the policies are followed, most parents readily accept this form of grouping. Presumably, grouping by age narrows the range of differences within each class, particularly when the teacher works with the entire class. Certain problems are encountered if the teacher does not recognize that grouping the children according to age will have no effect on the range of differences in other areas of behavior or performance. The conflict between the individual and the group still exists. The children have different life styles, different interests, and need different kinds of learning support. To be effective, the teacher still needs to provide for a wide range of differences.

Age grouping is probably most convenient for preschool groups, since many actually consist of children of only one age. Programs which have only four-year-olds do not really have much choice, but programs which have both three-year-olds and four-year-olds or four-year-olds and five-year-olds could make different arrangements.

Interage Groups

Within the last few years, grouping children together whose ages extend over a two- or three-year span has gained popularity, especially in Montessori Schools and in schools modeled after the British Infant Schools. Sometimes a term such as "family grouping" is used, based on the principle that the younger children learn from the older children and the older children help the younger children, as they do in families. Such a grouping deliberately creates a class in which children of different abilities are placed together, increasing the possibility that more individualization of instruction will take place. Because the differences in the children are so apparent, such grouping tends to break down some of the barriers to individual instruction created by tradition. Interaction between older and younger children helps younger children to look to the older children as models of behavior. It helps to establish feelings of accomplishment among the children as they become the oldest in the group and can contribute to the learning of the younger children. It can also be true that older children come to respect the efforts of younger children and that younger children are included in the activities of older children when they have something to contribute. Younger children often can progress faster in this kind of group than they can in a single age group.

Other Kinds of Grouping

A possibility for grouping that has been tried very little, but which seems to have promise, utilizes the prior experience of preschool children. Commonly, under the usual age grouping, a few children start school at age three, other children start at age four, and still more children start at age five. Each year some children without school experience are added to a class of children who have had experience the year before. During the initial period of adjustment for the new children, those who have been in school before are given very little that is new to them. Certainly it is true that the experienced children help the inexperienced children, but often little stimulation is offered to them at this time. Where there are several kindergartens in a school system, one kindergarten could be formed of children with previous nursery school experience, rather than ignoring the existence of such experience. These children should be able to engage in creative activities and problem solving beyond that expected of children who are just beginning to learn to participate in group activities.

Some schools form transition groups of children who have had kindergarten but who have been designated as not yet ready for the curriculum of first grade. This is a form of achievement grouping consistent with the policies of schools which have first grade classes formed on the basis of reading-readiness achievement.

Such groups are comfortable for teachers who expect children to be "ready" for the instruction which they plan to give them. If allowed to proceed into first grade, many of the children would be unable to succeed. It is better to provide this year of informal learning experiences than to let them fail.

Various team arrangements are sometimes implemented to achieve better use of school facilities or teacher abilities. Sometimes the classroom area is open construction, permitting use of wide areas by a larger group of children than would usually be in one class. Within the large area, smaller areas are created and the children are allowed to move freely from one area to another. The teachers plan together for supervision of the various areas, sometimes making use of their special abilities or interests. Often several part-time teachers can be incorporated into the team at intervals, increasing the variety of activities available to the children. The success of such team teaching is dependent on the organizational ability of the head teacher and the compatibility of the different team members. Under the direction of a very good team, children could have more varied experiences in this kind of group.

A limited amount of experimentation is being done with groups which are created for stated purposes. Some such groups are created to bring together children of different nationalities, racial groups, and socio-economic levels. When this is done the demand for human-relations skills among the staff is particularly great, and the involvement of parents is essential to facilitate relationships among the children. Opportunities exist to form such groups of children in rapidly changing neighborhoods and redeveloped areas. Sometimes public housing projects provide the setting for this kind of group. The early childhood program may become an avenue through which many groups associate with one another to enrich the program for the children and increase the community feeling among people of widely differing backgrounds.

Class Size

In determining class size, the general principle is the younger the children, the smaller the ratio of children to each adult and the smaller the number of children with which each child should have contact. When children of the same age are grouped together, fifteen is usually regarded as the largest number of three-year-olds that should be in one class. A class of four-year-olds might be as large as twenty, and a class of five-year-olds as large as twenty-five. Ideally, groups of four-year-olds should be limited to about eighteen, and groups of five-year-olds to twenty. While the number of children provides one basis for limiting class size, space also can be very important.

Open classrooms, especially designed so that children can divide themselves into small groups, and in which all the children never need be together in one spot, enable different concepts of class size. Here one must also consider the ratio of adults to children and the amount of space allowed per child. Provision must be made for adequate supervision of all the space that children use, as well as for adequate staff to meet the needs of the children.

Supervision of the youngest children in "open spaces" presents some unique problems. One must be certain that space is never left unsupervised and that children cannot wander away. It is especially important that children be able to identify with one adult who is consistently there.

ATTENDANCE

Children can benefit from the opportunities offered by an early childhood education program only if they attend regularly. Most parents realize this and make every effort to have the children attend regularly, but a few parents regard attendance more casually and find excuses to keep the child at home for the day.

Importance of Regular Attendance

Every teacher of young children has had a child in her class who came to school one day and stayed at home the next, or who was in school for a week and was out the next week or two. Sometimes these absences are for valid reasons such as illness; sometimes the reasons for absence are difficult to pinpoint. Schools encourage parents to keep ill children at home, yet some parents are so overly cautious that they keep their children home for illness when the child is not really ill. Other children are allowed to come to school when they really should be kept home. Each case must be worked out with the parent. The child who comes to school regularly builds friendships with the other children and looks forward to seeing them each morning. They play together regularly, have the usual squabbles, gain experience in settling them, and share new skills and knowledge. The child who is absent frequently feels strange and disoriented, because during his absence the other children move ahead with new activities and new relationships.

Early childhood programs have an ongoing, evolving program which requires full participation if the child is to derive the greatest value from it. There is a carry-over of interests from one day to the next. Children have some projects which continue for more than one day. The teacher often plans ahead with the children from one day to the next. A child may participate in all the planning for a trip, then miss the trip, or he may miss the planning and arrive back at school on the day of the trip. In this case he misses the fun of anticipating what is going to happen, and he also misses much of the knowledge to be gained. He misses the feeling of being a part of the group, which is important in any class, no matter what the age of the children.

Helping Parents with Attendance Problems

Some parents regard the nursery school or day care center as a convenience to them. It is thought of as a parking place for the child when the parent does not want him under foot. Some parents have ambivalent feelings about enrolling the child in school in the first place. They may feel that they are shirking their responsibility as parents by sending their child to school. The mother may feel lonesome and useless at home without her child, and she may find ways to justify keeping him at home with her. If the mother is going to be at home all day and doesn't want to make the effort to get up on time, she may just keep the child at home. She may really feel that her family is growing up and no longer needs her, so she wants to keep this child dependent on her. Sometimes there are problems involving a parent's feelings about the program of the school. The child may not be having the kind of experiences the parent had hoped he would, so she dismisses the program as unimportant. Continuous communication with the parent may be necessary to find out what the real feelings are and to work out solutions. It may be better for the child to stay at home all the time than to come to school irregularly.

Not Wanting to Go to School

Experienced nursery school teachers know that early in the year many children will explore "not wanting to go to school." This is of concern to both teachers and parents because it can be disrupting to both the school situation and the family routine. It can mean that something disturbing to the child has happened at school, although teachers and parents may not be able to identify an experience which could be the cause. This may happen when both parents and teachers have every evidence that the child really likes school. It is part of the transition that the child must make towards accepting school on his own, rather than because his parents insist.

Not wanting to go to school is most surprising when it comes from a child who started to school with great enthusiasm, went happily for a week or two, then suddenly refused to go. The parent is certain something terrible has happened at school, questions the child, but can find out nothing from him. The parent then questions the teacher, but she hasn't a clue. Once at school the child is fine—that is, if he gets there. At this point parental action is crucial in helping the child accept school.

Parents should try to give the child some understanding of what they think. They send him to school because it is a place to learn and they want him to learn as much as possible. Parents should explain to the child that father has his job, mother has her work to do, and he has his job, too—going to school. It may not even hurt to tell him that his father goes to work to earn money so that the family can do many things, including sending him to school. The explanation should be simple but matter of fact. Parents can be accepting of the fact that he doesn't want to go right now but this doesn't really change the fact that he is expected to go.

Parents should avoid a lot of questioning about what happens at school and why he doesn't want to go. The matter should not become the topic of conversation at the dinner table; older siblings should not be allowed to tease him about it. The home life should be pleasant, and there should be interesting things for the child to do after he comes home from school. Parents should never bribe him to go. Sometimes it is helpful to work out a different method of going to school. He may go more happily if he rides with his father as he goes to work, or he may find it better to walk with an older sibling. Going to school should be made as pleasant as possible, and the child might be permitted to take something from home, such as a suitable book or record to share with the class. The teacher should be supportive of the parent's efforts and do all she can to make school inviting to him.

A look at some of the events which may be going on in the family may also provide a clue to the child's not wanting to go to school. Has the family recently moved, or are they planning to move? Has the mother just taken a job, or is she planning to take one? Is there a new baby in the family, or is there a younger child who stays at home with the mother all day? Has grandmother come to visit? Is there anything different about the family routine that would cause the child to want to stay home? Are the child's usual playmates also in school, and does he know that they are not at home? Questions like these may suggest possible answers.

Just because the teacher does not know of any event that could have caused a negative feeling toward school doesn't mean that there hasn't been one. There may be something about school that the child very much dislikes. He may be afraid of another child. Maybe his mother was late calling for him one day, and he thought she was not coming. Maybe an animal on the playground frightened him. Once the teacher is aware of the problem, she may be able to observe situations which help to clarify the child's behavior.

If parents are ambivalent about having the child go to school it may contribute to the problem. The mother who doubts whether she should have enrolled the child may have a hard time when he doesn't want to go. Unless she has the courage to follow up on her decision, she and the child may be in for some difficult times. When the facts are considered, a preschool child does not have the judgment to decide whether he should go to school or not. Making decisions like this is a job for the responsible parent. Asking the child whether he wants to go or not is just begging for trouble.

QUESTIONS FOR DISCUSSION

1. Plan a talk to be given to parents who will enroll their children in kindergarten when it opens in the fall. How would you change this talk if it were to be given to parents of nursery school children?

2. A parent has come to you for advice on whether to enroll her child in the nursery school in which you are teaching. What questions would you raise with her? On what basis would you try to help her make her decision?

3. At what age do you think children should be enrolled in school? Why would you select this particular age?

4. What particular advantages do you see in grouping children of the same age together? Under what conditions would you favor inter-age grouping?

5. How would you handle the problem of a child who continuously comes to school late? How would you deal with irregular attendance?

6 Health and Safety Policies

A SAFE, WELL-RUN SCHOOL COMES ABOUT THROUGH THE planning and careful management of the school environment to create a healthful living situation. Both school and teachers should take care to plan a curriculum that fosters physical development. Children can hardly benefit from sunshine and fresh air if there is no place where they can safely get outside to enjoy it, or if the teacher does not allow them to go outdoors. Playground equipment may be the best in the world for developing strong bodies, but if no time is allowed in the schedule to go outdoors and climb on it, the value is not obtained. The teacher must guide the children in the routines essential to physical health and help them to use equipment in ways that are safe.

RESPONSIBILITY FOR SAFETY

When the owners of a nursery school occupy a facility and enroll children, they establish a relationship recognized by law. They assume certain responsibilities by the very act of opening a school. The same is true of a teacher who accepts a job in a nursery school. The administration and staff are liable for the health and safety of the children and, if legally challenged, must provide a suitable explanation for the way they handle this responsibility.[1] Nursery school liability is different from that of other schools because of the age of the children. When a child as young as four years is injured, there is deemed to be no contributory negligence on his part. His safety is the responsibility of the adult.

1. Robert D. Hess and Doreen J. Croft, *Teachers of Young Children* (Boston: Houghton Mifflin Company, 1972), p. 283.

Legally, nursery schools are places that care for children. The precautionary safety measures that the school takes must increase as the child's capacity to take care of himself decreases. Parents may sign a waiver but this does not release the teacher or director from liability. From a psychological point of view, however, it is a good idea to require signed permission slips for field trips and emergency treatment. This allows the parent to make a decision to keep the child at home if he objects to the child's going.

If injuries occur because of negligence, the school would have to prove its innocence. If this criterion does not apply, the burden would remain upon the child and his parents to demonstrate that the school staff was careless.[2] Circumstances could make a difference in the liability of a teacher. For example, if a child with a generally pleasant temperament injures another child, and the teacher is exercising proper supervision, the teacher would not be liable because the event would be completely unforeseen. If the teacher knows that a child has a tendency to hurt other children, however, she is liable if she does not protect the other children. The school could be held liable for accidents caused by defective equipment, but if reasonable precautions are taken, the teacher probably would not be held liable for a child's carelessness. The teacher is liable for injuries due to her own carelessness.[3]

Prevention is a teacher's best strategy in providing for the safety of the children. Careful maintenance of equipment, removal of all foreign objects such as glass and debris from the playground, and enforcement of safety rules do much to protect the children. The teacher must learn to be alert to both indoor and outdoor areas that present potential danger and to station herself where she can be accessible to those spots. She must particularly learn to be aware of the potential behavior of individual children in the group and anticipate quick dangerous moves by some children.

The School's Safety Program

A great many steps can be taken to protect the children who are enrolled in any program, as well as to protect the teachers should they become involved in legal action.

2. *Ibid.*, p. 285.
3. *Ibid.*, p. 287.

Planning the Environment. A well-planned environment helps to reduce the chance of accidents. Guidelines for planning safe surroundings are usually a part of the local and state health and sanitation regulations pertaining to nursery schools or day care centers. These codes vary from one state or local area to another, so it is necessary to consult the regulatory agency to find out the exact regulations. Standards for nursery schools and kindergartens are most often administered through state departments of education, while day care programs are more likely to fall under the jurisdiction of the department of welfare. Any owner or operator of a program that fails to meet these standards not only risks the safety of the children but also takes upon himself unnecessary responsibility for liability.

Safety measures associated with buildings and physical facilities have been discussed in Chapter 4, but those of special importance will be repeated here. If children are transported, there should be designated loading zones, off-street loading, and adequate parking areas. Premises should be well drained and free of insects and rodents. Outdoor play areas should be fenced. Gates should be provided which the children cannot open, and the play areas should be directly accessible to the indoor rooms. All fences, gates, and play equipment should be inspected regularly for splintered edges, rusty protruding parts, loose or pointed parts, and paint which contains more than one percent lead. Climbing equipment should be over soft grass, sandy surfaces, or an artificially created soft surface. Equipment beyond the developmental competence of the children constitutes a major hazard. Younger children should be protected from the more violent activities of older children, either by having separate play areas or by using the play area at different times.

All buildings used for schools must meet the fire and safety requirements of local and state agencies. Careful attention must be given to the safety of the heating system, prevention of burns from exposed radiators or heaters, protecting stairs with low railings, and providing adequate exits with doors opening outward.

Incidental Safety Teaching. The teacher does much incidental safety teaching. She consistently models behavior which she wishes the youngest children to observe, such as wiping up spills, closing doors carefully, and putting broken toys away to be repaired. With nursery school children she will often verbalize what she is doing to protect the children. If she picks up a board with a nail in it, she will say to the children who happen to be nearby, "Let's put that in the trash barrel; it could hurt us." Frequently she lets the children assist or take full responsibility, if the task is simple. She shows appreciation for the child's efforts by a comment such as, "Good, you put the board where no one can get hurt by it." When spills occur, the teacher helps children to get sponges and clean up. The teacher reinforces the action by indicating that the spill has been cleaned up so no one can slip and fall. These are examples of ways children can be guided to learn to handle the safety problems that arise. Some other things that nursery school and kindergarten children can learn to do are telling the teacher about broken glass, closing doors they open, turning off faucets they turn on, and playing out of the path of passersby.

Helping Children Learn to Live Safely. Learning to live safely begins very early when children learn not to touch something hot or to go up and down steps. Children of four or five years of age, however, still are not expected to be able to take full responsibility for their own safety. Although they may have been carefully drilled to look in both directions before crossing the street, a ball rolling across the street or a friend on the other side of the street may be enough to cause them to forget.

The school offers many opportunities for learning to play safely. Children who come to school in cars need to know the safe way to get in and out of the car and how to behave when riding in the car. On the playground, slides, swings, and other equipment can be dangerous when used carelessly but relatively safe when precautions are taken. The same is true for objects such as scissors, hammers, saws, hoes, rakes, shovels, pins and needles. The teacher demonstrates the use of equipment, offers reminders to the child regarding its use, and as a last resort stops a child from using equipment that he is misusing. She removes a child who is throwing sand from the sandbox; she removes a child from the jungle-gym who is pushing other children; or she takes a hammer about to be aimed at a friend. Some people feel that children should not use potentially dangerous equipment; however, a much more justifiable approach seems to be to teach the child how to use it safely. For the most part, young children are surprisingly responsive to the trust of adults and take pride in knowing how to use real tools or to climb safely.

As another safety precaution, preschool children need to know how to give an adult the information needed to help them. As children begin to move out of the home environment, they need to know their names and addresses and the names of their parents. As soon as they start to school they should learn the name of the school they attend. When they become interested in numbers they can learn their telephone number.

A kindergarten child who walks to school by himself must be taught not to accept rides with strangers. This is a difficult thing for adults to teach because generally they want children to learn to trust people. To call attention to the fact that there are people who cannot be trusted is difficult without frightening a child. Parents who do permit children to walk to school alone should be certain that a crossing guard is always on duty and that someone is always at home when the child returns. It should be clear to the child that he is expected to come directly home from school.

Many five-year-olds should not be permitted to go to school alone under any circumstances, and four-year-olds are seldom able to handle that much freedom even though they may very much want to. Location of the school and the home are very important factors in deciding what the child should be allowed to do. If a staff knows that undesirable people are sometimes found on the streets or even in the school building, they will encourage caution on the part of parents and hope that it will be heeded. Sometimes under these circumstances it is not possible for a child to have the freedom he might be able to handle in less dangerous circumstances.

Handling Accidents

Records regarding health and illness should be kept up to date. The information regarding who to call in case of illness or accident and who is responsible for the child when he is not in school, as well as who is authorized to pick up the child, should be readily available in case of an emergency. The school should have a record of any special restrictions on the child's diet or physical activity. Written reports should be prepared routinely of any illnesses or injuries that occur at school. Illnesses and injuries should be reported to parents, even though they may seem minor at the time, along with any first-aid action taken.

A comprehensive insurance program must cover the teachers as well as the owners of a school in case of unavoidable accidents. The consequences of a serious accident can be tragic for the teacher or director, as well as for the child and his family.

It is reassuring that such serious accidents seldom happen and the teacher with good training need not feel apprehensive if reasonable precautions are taken. Most teachers can deal effectively with situations that arise if procedures on what to do have been clarified.

HEALTH

Policies related to the health of the children should be formulated and made available to parents and all personnel. To be effective, policies should be consistently enforced and should be supplemented with policies regarding the health of staff and other persons who come in contact with the children.

Medical Examinations and Medical Care

When a child has been enrolled in a nursery school or kindergarten program, he should be examined by a physician prior to the date he enters school. This examination should determine whether the child is physically ready to participate in the school activities or whether limitations should be placed on his participation. Forms for this examination are usually sent to the parent for the child's doctor. After the doctor has completed the forms, he returns them to the school. A policy should be developed which includes specifications about when the examination must be made. An examination made too far in advance of school entry cannot take into account recent developments. Usually the specified time varies from one month before school entry to two weeks after entry.

At the time that the examination is made, the child should be immunized against such communicable diseases as whooping cough, diphtheria, measles, and poliomyelitis. Because most children are apt to get occasional scrapes and scratches, they should be protected against tetanus. Most physicians no longer recommend smallpox vaccinations. The school's policies for immunization may be based on recommendations of the local public health department.

Medical opinion varies as to the value of physical examinations, although they are required by most schools. It is felt that these examinations are often superficial and do not reveal problems not already known by the parents. But there remain many children who have never been seen by a physician or who would benefit from thorough and competent examination. Discontinuation of the examination hardly seems the solution, as it often is the vehicle through which the school gains its information.

Head Start and other federally-funded programs require that a physical examination be provided for each child in the program. Many of these children have not had previous medical examinations. Examination of these children does sometimes uncover serious medical problems which have been allowed to go untreated.

Meeting the health and medical problems of children who have not had regular medical care presents a very different problem from meeting the health needs of children who have been under regular medical care prior to school entrance. Private schools and cooperative nursery schools have usually seen the medical examination as a safeguard for the protection of the health of the child who is enrolled and the other children. If medical problems exist, responsibility for treatment is assumed by the family. Head Start and some day care programs in deprived areas do assume the responsibility for providing treatment for problems discovered during the physical examination. Simply informing a parent that his child needs treatment seldom results in the correction of a problem. Other steps are necessary. The parent must be present at the time of the health evaluation, and the physician must explain the nature of the health program, the need for treatment, and the nature of the treatment needed. Often someone from the program—the physician, nurse, social worker, or health aide—must help the parent find the necessary services and funds to pay for the services. Often this person may need to see that the parent and child have transportation to the physician or clinic and that other children are cared for while the parent is away. The health records must be continually reviewed to ensure that the recommended treatment is actually taking place.

In programs where Federal funds are provided for treatment, it becomes the joint responsibility of the day care director and the physicians and other health personnel to see to the treatment and follow-up. The administrator must provide funds and services to enable the family to arrange transportation and baby sitting. Screening tests and examinations must be scheduled so that the results are available to the examining physician at the time he makes the recommendations for health care.

A nursery school or day care program seldom has the funds to provide the services necessary to remedy existing health problems and prevent the occurrence of new ones. Usually priorities must be set in health services. Guidelines usually give first priority to acute conditions requiring immediate treatment to alleviate symptoms or to prevent disability. High priority is also given for conditions which may be progressive if untreated and which interfere with classroom functions and require either corrective treatment or special classroom programming. Low priority is recommended for certain commonly performed medical procedures which have never been scientifically shown to improve the health of children, such as repair of umbilical hernias, tonsillectomy, and adenoidectomy.[4] If at all possible, the health evaluation and care that is provided while the child is in the program should be performed by a physician or clinic that will continue to care for the child, even though the child is no longer enrolled in the day care program. The health evaluation alone may be worth very little to children whose families, either through apathy or lack of funds, fail to provide the remedial treatment.

Illnesses of Young Children

Because young children are highly susceptible to illness, policies should be developed to protect the health of children who participate in educational programs. Parents who think that a child gets more colds and illnesses when he first goes to nursery school are probably right. This happens because of the exposure to many new children, rather than because of the nursery school program

4. A. Frederick North, *Day Care Health Services*, No. 6 in Child Development Series on Day Care (Washington, D.C.: Office of Child Development, 1971), p. 13.

itself. This is likely to happen the first year the child goes to school, whether it is nursery school, kindergarten, or first grade, because of exposure to more children. As the child builds up immunity to the different viruses and illnesses, the chance of illness is reduced.

The Common Problem of Colds. The cold is the most persistent problem of preschool children. Parents often send the child to school despite the fact that the child has a cold. When the child is present in the group, he infects other children and the teacher. No matter how hard a school tries, it is very difficult to prevent this happening.

Colds are a problem in the classroom. Any child with a runny nose and a cough is disturbing to the teacher. The younger the child, the greater the problem. Teachers try to teach children to cover their mouths and turn away their heads when they cough, but there is no way to be entirely successful.

Some doctors seem to feel that colds are not communicable after the first few days and after the child has no fever. Nursery school teachers, however, are not easily convinced of this. All will agree that it is difficult to tell when a cold is contagious, and often children are in school when teachers definitely feel they should not be there. Most schools succeed in keeping the very sick child at home, but where colds are concerned the child may often be sent to school.

Tuberculosis. While tuberculosis may not seem like a major health problem today, it nevertheless concerns physicians, educators, and public health authorities. About 1.5 percent of four million children in the United States entering school at six years of age are positive tuberculin reactors. Since a positive tuberculin test in a preschool child usually denotes active disease, many cases of tuberculosis will originate from this group. Yearly testing is recommended from the age of four to six and one-half years, and after that biannual testing.[5] Tuberculin testing of all teachers, assistants, and especially kitchen staff is also essential.

5. David H. Weintraub, "The Preschool Child: Health Concepts," Chapter V in *Early Childhood Education*, Seventy-first Yearbook of the National Society for the Study of Education, ed. Ira J. Gordon (Chicago: University of Chicago Press, 1972), p. 75.

Communicable Diseases. Policies regarding communicable diseases should establish procedures to be followed when a child or teacher has been exposed to a communicable disease, the length of time a child should stay out of school, and on what authority he is readmitted to school. These policies are usually the same as those set by local public health authorities. Charts giving essential information about communicable diseases are readily available from the local health department or from the state health department. Often copies can be obtained for parents.

Teachers should become aware of symptoms of communicable disease and should notify parents when children have been exposed to an infectious illness. Although the teacher will be able to do little in the school setting, teachers and parents working together may be able to avert the spread of the disease. A disease such as German measles is a special hazard because of the danger to mothers in the early months of pregnancy. Recognizing the danger that this disease poses to young families, routine immunization is often recommended before a child enters nursery school, as is the immunization of young female teachers of child-bearing age.

Emergency Care

Most medical problems which occur during the usual school day are minor and can be handled by the staff, preferably by someone trained in first-aid. While teachers or directors of private schools often take care of minor difficulties, public schools often prohibit teachers from applying medication of any kind. Teachers must be aware of what they may legally do.

The most frequent medical problems in early childhood programs are slight cuts, skinned knees, and bumped heads. The usual treatment consists of a calm examination of the child to see that he is not seriously hurt, along with comfort and reassurance from the teacher. The teacher, of course, will see that the wound is clean and apply a bandage if the skin is broken. In many cases, a bandage satisfies the injured child's psychological need. To young children, the band-aid is a status symbol, and they will endure minor pain in order to wear one.

Hopefully, all of the situations that the teacher will face are of the minor variety. If not, procedures to follow must be clear.

There are emergencies, such as fractures, animal bites, large lacerations, eye injuries, and sudden high fevers, which can usually be handled temporarily by a responsible person who makes the patient comfortable while a nurse or physician can be called. Medical assistance should be available within ten or twenty minutes. There is time to notify parents and ask their wishes about a source of medical care. The physician or clinic who usually cares for the child may be contacted for advice. If they cannot be reached, the child should be transported directly to a source of medical care.

Certain severe emergencies such as electrical shock, obstruction of the respiratory tract, massive external hemorrhage, and internal poisoning require the immediate intervention of someone trained in first aid or emergency medical care. "Whatever life saving measures are necessary should be applied by whoever is present and has a knowledge of first aid or emergency medical care."[6] The child then should be transported to a treatment center as promptly as possible.

Children with true medical emergencies such as internal bleeding, penetrating and crushing injuries of the chest, unconsciousness, heat stroke, severe or extensive burns, and snake bites should be transported immediately to a hospital emergency room or other emergency treatment facility. For such emergency conditions, no time should be wasted in trying to obtain the services of a nurse or physician or in locating parents. The first action should be to obtain emergency transportation; the second action should be to call the hospital or treatment facility and alert it to the condition of the child being sent. Only after these measures have been taken should other interested parties be called.

The Nurse in Early Childhood Programs

It is desirable to have a nurse in charge of the health program of a school, especially if children come from families which need help in health care. The school should also be able to obtain the services of a pediatrician when needed. One of his chief services would be consulting with the nurse, who would have direct contact with the children. Often problems arise in which a doctor's

6. A. Frederick North, p. 40.

opinion is needed; it is of great assistance if he can be reached quickly by telephone. The nurse can help with the food and sanitation problems of the school as well as work with the children and the parents. Responsibility for health records is rightfully hers, and she should report any unusual circumstances to the director and staff.

The routine for morning inspection is usually established by the nurse. Each day she will examine the child's eyes, nose, throat, mouth, chest, hands and arms for any unusual redness or rash, giving special attention to any child who has been sick. This routine usually means that the person bringing the child to school must wait until the child has been checked in and admitted to the group. Often having a nurse on duty will deter a parent from bringing a sick child to school before he has fully recovered; the parent will not run the risk of being asked to take the child home. Parents who have daily contact with the nurse learn to look to her for guidance in dealing with the health problems of their children.

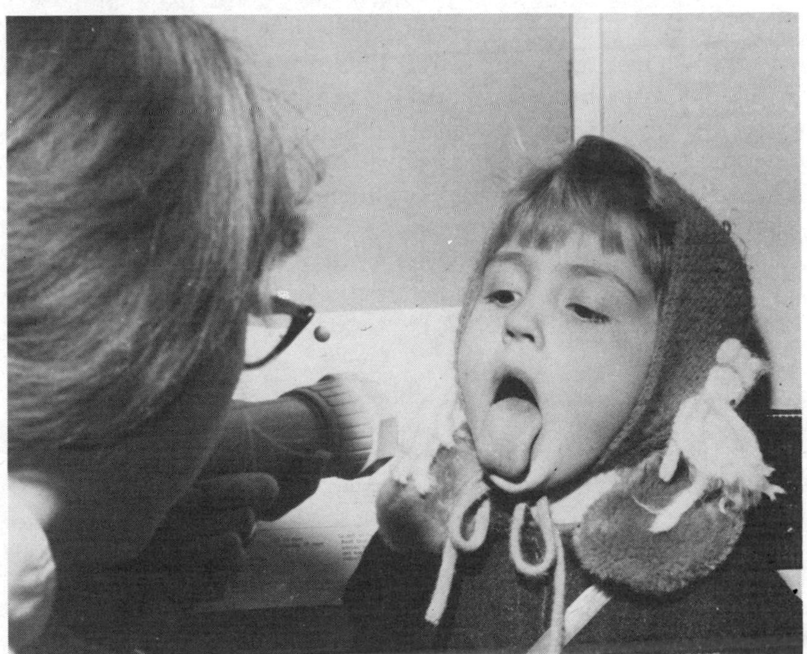

Courtesy of Educational Facilities Laboratories and M. Swayze

In addition to morning inspection and consultation with parents, the nurse will usually be the person who informs parents that children have been exposed to communicable diseases, the symptoms the parents should watch for, and how to protect their children from the disease. She will help them understand the function of the health policies of the school. She will do the systematic screening of vision, speech and hearing, and make recommendations to staff and parents about correcting defects that might interfere with learning when the child reaches school age. Children will be weighed and measured regularly, with records kept to show the gains made. The child's height and weight will be reported to the parents, and parents will be consulted if there is any wide deviation from the child's usual pattern of growth.

The school staff is always concerned about children who are ill and unable to be in school. In the case of extended illness or repeated illness causing irregular attendance, the nurse will contact the family to discuss the child's problems. While it is usually expected that parents will contact the school when the children are to be absent, the nurse may make the call if they do not. In this way she will help to encourage regular attendance and will be aware of the physical problems that may prevent the child from coming to school. Sometimes this contact is sufficient to cause parents otherwise careless about attendance to see that their children get to school. This contact may also encourage the overprotective parent to send a child to school when he really should be there. The nurse's knowledge of the children and their families is invaluable. She can make recommendations to parents on the basis of her previous observation and experience.

Health Information

Much health information about the child is directly obtainable from the parent and can be helpful to the director of the school. It is essential to know who to contact in case of an emergency and how to contact them as quickly as possible. Parents can supply information about the child's previous health history and his early physical development. Knowing the diseases the child has already had helps the nurse to assess the effect of exposure to communicable diseases. Many health problems that young children have do not necessarily exclude them from school, but parents should inform the school of any special restrictions and should give the school as much additional information as possible. Often both parents and doctors want a child to be treated normally, and little adjustment of the program is necessary.

One of the most frequently needed kinds of information is whether the child is permitted to participate in swimming or water play involving a wading pool or sprinkler during summer programs. Because of repeated colds, ear infections, or sore throats parents and doctors sometimes do not want a child to participate under any circumstances.

Whether or not a child goes outside to play may also depend on information from parents. Schools usually assume that children well enough to be in school are well enough to go outside to play for a short time. Programs usually have an outdoor time even when the weather is quite cold. Parents who feel that the child should not be outdoors for a short time will usually need to make special arrangements with the school. It is reasonable to expect a school to see that children have coats, caps, mittens and boots on, if they have worn them to school. Children may also stay out for shorter periods than others. Very active children are seldom bothered by the cold and keep themselves warm through their activity, whereas the quieter children get cold sooner. The teacher will initiate some running games or active play but she should consider the length of time it is wise for these children to stay outside. When a class has more than one teacher, all children need not stay outside for the same length of time. A kindergarten teacher who does not have the assistance of an aide is very limited in the concessions she can make for individual children. She can neither leave children outside nor send them inside without someone to supervise them. In any situation where teachers work as teams, it is possible to be flexible, so that some children are outside with one teacher and some are inside with other teachers. This can be done safely as long as the teachers are aware of the comings and goings of the children, and fences and easy access to the classroom provide maximum safety.

Screening Tests

Screening tests should be carried out for all preschool children. Such tests do not represent a complete evaluation, but they identify a group of children who require more complete professional evaluation. The everyday program should incorporate measurement of physical growth, vision, and hearing. Other forms of screening may be carried out by individual programs, depending on the population of children served and the prevalence of health problems.

Assessment of Physical Growth. Any teacher or parent can weigh and measure the child, recording the data on the growth chart. Weight should be measured on a beam balance scale. Height should be measured with the child standing with his back to a wall on which a measure has been mounted. Care should be taken to have a straight-edged device, such as a ruler, rested against the child's head at a right angle to the measure.

Vision Screening. The most appropriate vision screening test can often be determined by consultation with an eye specialist who will be responsible for evaluation and treatment of children selected by the screening tests. Health departments and school health programs may have established procedures which may be applied to older preschool children. If assistance cannot be obtained from either of these sources, the National Society for the Prevention of Blindness may be contacted.[7] Testing is usually performed by nurses, health aides, or volunteers trained in the method. The Snellen Illiterate E Visual Testing Chart is frequently used with children over age three. They can be taught to play the "E game" and will permit their eyes to be covered with the occluder. This test can be set up in a quiet place in the school and easily administered.

Hearing Test. Children can be tested with an audiometer after age three. The teacher can prepare the children for the test by demonstrating the procedure in the classroom, allowing the children to become familiar with the sounds and to learn the desired responses. School health programs and health departments probably have both the testing equipment and the personnel trained for its use. It is usually more economical for small schools to obtain the services from a trained technician in a larger program than to try to provide their own.

7. *Ibid.*, p. 21.

MENTAL HEALTH

Health and health personnel are usually concerned with the child's mental as well as his physical health and well-being. This concern often creates close ties between the nursery school or kindergarten and the child's physician. Physicians quite often recommend nursery schools to parents when they feel that the school can perform a service needed by the family. Recommendations may be made on the basis of the child's need for opportunities for relationships with others outside his immediate family. As the child moves into the world of school, a feeling of acceptance by other children and by the school personnel is essential for his mental health. He needs to learn to share toys and play equipment, and to modify some of his individualistic behavior in accordance with the minimum requirements for group relations. As the conflicts are many among preschool children, much of the incidental teaching done by the teacher consists of her guidance of children in conflict situations. The school should make an attempt to provide a setting with as few frustrations for the children as possible, yet to eliminate all frustrations is recognized as an impossibility. Children at preschool age are just learning the skills of living together. Planning for this kind of learning is one of the most important tasks of the teacher. It calls for special skills beyond those required for teachers of older children.

Many of the standard practices of good early childhood programs are considered important in preventive mental health. Programs which aim to cultivate a positive self-image in the child and which provide a warm accepting human environment have attributes of mental health services. Children who might not be able to adjust to a regular school classroom can benefit from the small classes and the high staff to child ratio of another program. Often children with physical or intellectual handicaps can be given the care they require just as the "normal" children are given the care they require. Parent involvement is also an important aspect of the mental health program provided by the school. By observing other children and by discussing problems with teachers and other parents, a parent is often reassured that his child's problems are shared by other children.

It is desirable to have a psychiatrist or psychologist as a

consultant. His special knowledge can help the staff achieve successful experiences with each child and may help teachers interpret the behavior of children and modify undesirable behavior. He may also help teachers and aides be more comfortable with "difficult" parents and children. He may be particularly helpful in endorsing certain techniques used by the staff and in making recommendations to families whose children cannot adjust to the program.

SCHOOL PRACTICES AND HEALTH OF THE CHILDREN

Very little direct instruction in health is undertaken in nursery school and little more in kindergarten. Most teaching is done in connection with daily school routines and activities. Because this teaching is more incidental and could be easily overlooked by the teacher, occasional review of the school practices which relate to both physical and mental health should be carried out, and particular experiences identified which are important for the children. Teacher awareness of learning opportunities which are available to children often means the difference between a situation in which children are aware of learning and one in which the learning is overlooked.

School Practices

School routines should be planned to enable children to develop habits that will be used not only in school but at home as well. Washing hands can consume a good bit of time in nursery school because of the children's enjoyment of playing in the water. The teacher can demonstrate the correct way to wash and dry hands. She should be careful to remind children to wash after toileting, before lunch, and after painting or playing with clay.

Making children aware of proper clothing for the climate or the activity is frequently appropriate in connection with nursery school activity. Children wear smocks or old shirts to protect their clothing from paint and other messy activities. They wear warm clothing, caps, and mittens when it is very cold outside. Different clothing is worn inside and out when it is cold, and different clothing is worn to school and for parties. Children like to talk about

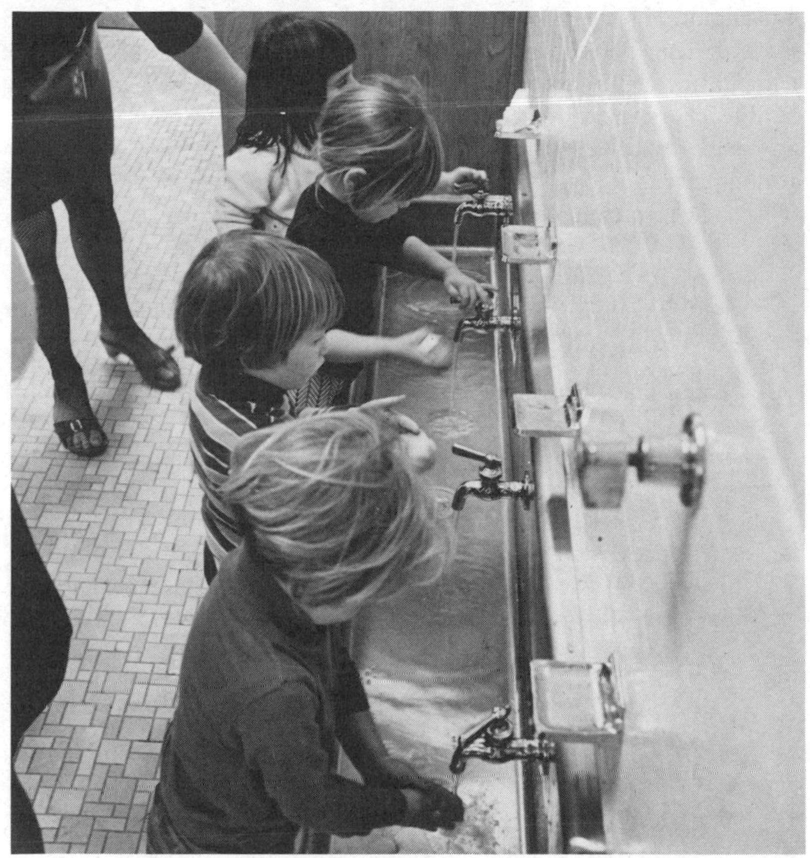

Courtesy of Educational Facilities Laboratories and Rondal Partridge

clothing. They easily understand the importance of wearing proper clothing under different circumstances.

The teacher must plan a program which balances rest and activity. For example, a relatively quiet time should be planned before lunch; children should rest after they have eaten their noon meal, although not all may actually sleep. The teacher can often allow for activity after children have been relatively quiet for a portion of time. Some children tend to become overstimulated and overactive during the school day, and the teacher may indicate to them that she is helping them find quieter activities until they can become calmer. The teacher can help a child do this without any implication of punishment or deprivation of privilege. At other times, she may simply respond to what seem to be the needs of the children without reference to a particular child. She may use this opportunity to point out to the children that they are tired of active play and need something more quiet for awhile. The teacher may also interpret the children's need for outdoor play.

Seeing that children get proper rest and sleep are often problems faced by parents. As children become more aware of the family activities that occur after they go to bed, they often refuse to go to bed. They begin to develop favorite television programs and want to stay up late enough to watch them. Parents and teachers will still have to take most of the responsibility for seeing that children get the proper balance between activity and rest. They can make it easier if they help children understand the reasons for their requests and the consequences when the child does not get proper rest.

Children are usually interested in their own bodies and can begin to learn how to take care of their bodies. They like to be weighed and measured and to know that they are growing. They enjoy experiences which involve using the sense organs. Experiences with sound, smell, sight, and touch help them to be aware of how these organs help them. As some kindergarten children begin to lose their baby teeth, interest in teeth becomes great and many opportunities for teaching arise, such as instruction in brushing teeth.

Opportunities for learning about food differ greatly with the program that is provided. Children in day care who have a hot lunch at school have many opportunities to learn about food and to eat foods that may not ordinarily be served in their homes. The importance of food may be greatly enhanced if children have an opportunity to help prepare it or if some new foods are introduced on a choice basis. Children in schools with shorter sessions can enjoy some of the same experiences with food in relation to their between-meal snack at school. Experiences with food should be made as enjoyable and as social as possible. The beginnings of social courtesy can be begun with the teacher saying "please" and "thank you" at appropriate times and helping the child to learn to swallow the food in his mouth before he talks. Children also enjoy

Courtesy of Educational Facilities Laboratories and George Zimbel

simple parties to which they invite their parents to share foods they have helped prepare. Often at school they can become acquainted with new foods and acquire a willingness to try new foods as well as familiar foods.

Prior to the time of school entrance, many children have had negative experiences with the doctor, dentist or other health personnel. One of the real advantages of having a nurse to inspect the children every morning is that they come to know her as a person and to regard to her as their friend. She does not give them a shot and do something that hurts when she inspects them. Schools can provide experiences such as a visit to the dentist's office when he shows the children his equipment and lets them try out his chair. They can hear stories about visiting doctors or hospitals which help them to understand what happens and why a child must have these experiences.

HEALTH EDUCATION FOR STAFF AND PARENTS

Good health programs go beyond the legal provisions for health and safety by providing health education programs for parents and by making provision for the staff's health and well-being.

Health of the Staff

Usual practice requires staff to supply a statement by a licensed physician regarding pre-employment physical and mental health conditions. It is also desirable for staff members to be immunized against communicable diseases. Immunizations that provide temporary immunity against such illnesses as flu or colds may also be required, as may immunizations against diseases to which they have been exposed. In case of illness, staff members should be required to remain away from work until they have fully recovered. Returning to work too soon may be hazardous to both the employee and the children in the school.

Legal requirements vary from one state to another, but the health program should require that all such requirements are met by all employees. Some positions, such as cooks and other food handlers, may be more strictly regulated than others. Policies should be developed which indicate whether all staff should comply with the strict standards.

Health policies should also include procedures and forms for dealing with injury to employees. Some programs will operate under agencies carrying workmen's compensation insurance policies and will have forms and procedures for reporting injuries. In addition to this, all programs will want to review all injuries, even those not reported to an insurance company, to assess the health and safety practices in the school.

Administering School Health Policies

Every staff member should be furnished with a copy of the school's health and safety regulations, developed by the governing board of the school. Every staff member should be familiar with his responsibilities in implementing the health program. In nonpublic schools it is a good policy for all staff members to receive training in how to administer first-aid, emphasizing what is to be done until competent medical aid can be obtained.

The administration of medication to children can create problems. The policies of programs lasting only two or two and one-half hours may prohibit the administration of medications, either those prescribed by the child's physician or medications such as aspirin. Such policies are sometimes justified on the basis that a child who needs medication more often than every two hours probably is not well enough to be in school. Problems are somewhat different in the day care center. Often prescribed medications for noncontagious medical problems are administered after meals or at other intervals which occur when the child is at the center. If children must receive prescribed medication while at the day care center, directions must be followed exactly. Those who administer it must know if medication must be given at a specific time to be effective. All medication should be kept in a locked compartment out of the reach of the children.

Helping Parents Understand the Health Program

The health program must involve parents in improving and maintaining the health and well-being of their children. Parents may need help in understanding why certain health or medical requirements exist, what they must do if children are exposed to communicable diseases, and the importance of diagnostic or treatment recommendations. They may need help in locating and using health services. Nutrition and its relation to the health and well-being of families should be emphasized in parent education, especially in programs in depressed areas.

QUESTIONS FOR DISCUSSION

1. Plan the health policies for a private nursery school that is in session for two half-day sessions daily, that has access to the services of a nurse, and has arrangements to consult with a physician whenever the need arises.

2. Write a statement of the health policies for a Head Start program located in a rural area which has very limited health facilities. How would you arrange for the services which would be needed by the children?

3. Make a list of the items a staff would want to include in making a safety survey of the facilities, equipment and program of the school.

4. Write guidelines for supervising the outdoor play activities of the children, providing for safe use of equipment and space.

5. Select several pieces of equipment either in the classroom or on the playground, and discuss their potential value in relation to the dangers that might arise from their use.

7 Managing School Finances

GOOD EARLY CHILDHOOD EDUCATION IS EXPENSIVE. BRINGING up children is expensive—and the cost to the community and the family is even greater in later years if the early years of childhood are neglected. These facts must continuously be repeated if children are to be the beneficiaries of good early childhood programs. Open ing and operating an early childhood program is a business arrangement, and anyone considering such a venture should enter into it informed about skills that are necessary to succeed. Any private individual who decides to open a nursery school or kindergarten must follow all established legal procedures for opening a business. The Internal Revenuc Service will expect him to be accountable for all money spent and received, just as in any other business.

HOW PROGRAMS ARE FINANCED

Public funds are not available for financing preschool programs on a widespread basis. Financing, therefore, is usually a problem that must be faced before any program becomes operational. The common sources used to finance a program are parents' fees, funds from local community chests or from other local fund-raising compaigns, government appropriations for special purposes or for specified populations, endowments, fund-raising by the particular program, and occasional special gifts.

Parents' Fees

The majority of nursery school programs and many day care centers are financed by parents' fees. Many kindergarten programs are also financed by the parents in states which do not allow state aid to kindergarten programs. Cooperative schools, private schools, and church-sponsored schools are largely financed by parents' fees. The fees which are assessed must be in accordance with the expected expenditures. Fees must provide the income which will be expended to run the program, usually allowing a small cushion for emergencies. Private schools as a rule are the most expensive, sometimes charging $800 to $1,000 for the year's tuition. Costs to the family are often cut by having groups of children that attend two days a week and groups that attend three days a week. Most private schools must obtain funds to provide the program as well as some profit for the owner. Often the quality of the program varies depending on the extent to which the owner is committed to good education for children compared to how interested he is in making a profit. Making a profit on an early childhood program is not easy because there are limits to the fees young families can afford to pay, and because good programs are expensive to operate. During the initial years of a program particularly, planning to make an appreciable profit is unrealistic.

The cooperative school is able to charge lower fees than the private school because of the contribution the parents make in services as assistant teachers and as officers, committee chairmen, and committee members. The church-sponsored school if it is also a cooperative school is likely to be the least expensive, as it frequently has both the contribution of services by parents and the contribution of space and sometimes equipment by the church. No profit is usually involved in either of these types of program, with the exception of the money the leadership thinks necessary to take care of emergencies, pay bills during the summer, and get the program going the following year. Such programs often maintain a small savings account for these purposes. The account helps each incoming group of parents feel secure in making a few purchases and financial commitments before the tuition for the year is paid.

Assessing fees for day care programs is a much more complex process. All parents with children in day care may not pay the same fee, because of differences in income; therefore, information about the family must be obtained before fees for an individual child can be determined. Several factors determine the fees paid to a day care center, including the auspices of the center, the financing available, and community attitudes toward working mothers and the care of young children outside the home. Fees are much related to the fact that public funds are not permanently available on a widespread basis. In many day care centers, fees must equal costs plus profit, if one is to be made. Even though some community support may be available, the community agency which supplies the support may expect the day care center to supply a part of its budget through its own efforts. There is also a prevailing point of view that parents should pay whatever they can afford.

Before setting fees, information has to be collected about operating costs, about the community, and about the families the program expects to serve. If a program already is in operation, its costs should be converted to a unit cost for care or a cost per child per day.[1] An accountant or auditor familiar with the program will be able to suggest an appropriate method for arriving at this figure by calculating the indirect costs such as utilities, payroll service, insurance, administrative salaries, office supplies and many others.

Community factors which affect the setting of fees are prevailing wage and salary rates, the cost of living, and the distribution of work opportunities by categories such as professional, technical, clerical, and unskilled. The fee schedule in a community having low wages and salaries, a low cost of living, and a large number of semiskilled workers would be lower than a fee schedule in a community where wages, salaries and the cost of living are higher, and a large number of persons are employed in professional and technical positions.

Situations vary enough so that each school's policy-making body will have to decide its own fee schedule to conform to particular requirements and conditions. Some decisions must be made in relation to: setting of fees for a family from which more than one child is enrolled; how fees should be computed, whether by the week, semi-monthly, or monthly; how absences should be treated; how delinquent accounts should be handled; how fees will be collected, where and by whom; how the money will be protected until it arrives at the bank or other respository.[2]

1. Malcolm S. Host and Pearl B. Heller, *Day Care Administration*, No. 7, Child Development Series (Washington, D.C.: Office of Child Development, 1971), pp. 133.
2. *Ibid.*, p. 134.

The policies regarding the collection and handling of fees must be consistent. The procedure should be business-like and receipts should be given to parents as fees are paid. Delinquent fee accounts should be reported promptly and not permitted to continue. Policies should call for prompt exploration of the causes of delinquency and may permit adjustments, especially in case of a partially subsidized day care program. Parents should be encouraged to correct delinquent accounts promptly so that the account does not grow to a size they feel they can never pay off.

Public Funds

Public funds for early childhood education are available largely for the support of kindergartens in public schools in states which have permissive laws. Very little public money has been made available to programs for four-year-olds. Some money is appropriated, through government agencies, for use with specific groups of preschool children who qualify, such as children of working mothers, children from low socio-economic backgrounds, and children of migrant workers. Since this money has limitations imposed on its use, only certain segments of the population are reached by it. This money may be available to public agencies such as the public schools, or it may be made available to private institutions which meet the criteria and the standards of the program. Growing recognition of the need for public programs available for all children is leading to widespread effort to pass legislation which would make funds available for this purpose.

Government agencies sometimes make specific contributions to early childhood programs through providing surplus food, free school lunches, and medical care. Also, space for day care centers is sometimes made available in public housing projects; other public space is made available to programs as an "in-kind" contribution.

Fund-Raising

Often early childhood programs benefit from an annual campaign for public support, such as the Community Chest Drive. Such funds usually do not fully support a program. They are more often designed to make up the difference between an agency's anticipated income from all other sources and its estimated annual expenses.

This is a fluctuating amount which must be negotiated each year and is at all times based on the total funds obtained during the drive. Such funds often enable day care programs to subsidize the fees paid by low-income families so that it is possible to set fees in accordance with the families' ability to pay.

Individual programs may also conduct fund-raising campaigns of their own. They may sponsor theater benefits, rummage sales, book fairs, bake sales, or card parties. Often such efforts are more satisfactory if the fund-raising event is planned to raise money for some specific purpose, such as a large, expensive piece of equipment or scholarships for children of low-income families. Some of these projects are well established in the community and have excellent support. Communities sometimes support these fund-raising ventures in recognition of the program's contribution to community life and its importance to children.

Endowments and Other Special Gifts

Some long-established day care programs and nursery school programs are fortunate enough to have continuing income from endowments or property belonging to the corporation. Usually such property has been acquired at the bequest of some individual or foundation that had a special interest in perpetuating the program. To have this source of income is very important to a program. It considerably reduces fees that must be charged to families it serves, particularly if many of these families cannot afford to pay the usual fees.

One-time gifts of small amounts of money for a specific purpose, such as money to supplement the equipment budget or to purchase a certain piece of equipment, are occasionally received by nursery schools and day care centers that are nonprofit. An individual may give money in memory of someone previously associated with the program, or may provide a scholarship for a child whose parents cannot afford to enroll him in the program. Such gifts are helpful if appropriately designated, but cannot be relied on to make a major contribution to actual operating expenses.

Occasionally programs are funded with research and development funds from private foundations, if the purpose of the project is to develop a certain type of program. Research funds may be obtained to support a specific project operating in conjunction with the program. Such funds would not actually support the program but could make it more stable through the research and recognition received.

THE COST OF OPERATING A SCHOOL

The plan for the school budget should be based on an estimate of actual expenditures. During the first year of operation, the estimates will not always be accurate for such costs as supplies and food. With records of actual expenditures, however, a more accurate budget can be prepared for the next year. Keeping accurate financial records is an important part of any business venture. If the person who is to keep the records has not had bookkeeping training or experience, he should obtain help in setting up the bookkeeping system and keeping it accurately. It should be possible to tell at any time how much money the school has, in each of its budget categories.

Some of the categories that should be included in a school budget are as follows:

1. Salaries, wages, and employee benefits.
2. Rent or mortgage payment.
3. Insurance.
4. Utilities—heat, light, water, and gas.
5. Food.
6. Educational equipment.
7. Educational supplies.
8. Household equipment.
9. Household supplies.
10. Office supplies.
11. Publicity.
12. Postage, telephone, and transportation.
13. Professional development.
14. Other services and goods.

Salaries

Salaries make up the largest single item in the school budget. Salaries may vary considerably from one community to another, but the proportion of the budget allocated to salary expenses is usually eighty percent or more.[3] Schools that want to be competitive in the selection of staff will find that their salaries must not lag far behind those of other schools. As the staff is the key to the quality of the program, there should be little economizing on staff, either in the number employed or in the quality of their professional competence.

In making estimates of salaries for budgets, payments for social security and any other retirement plans should be included. Unemployment insurance and medical and hospital insurance should also be included if applicable. An allowance should be provided for normal salary increments according to the policy adopted by the school's board or director. Salary estimates must also include funds to pay substitutes in case of absence or during vacations.

Rent or Mortgage Payment

The second largest expense in the operation of a school is housing, unless some of the funds for housing can be obtained as an in-kind contribution. If a building is to be purchased for the school, a sum of money will be needed for a down payment, and possibly for repairs or alterations to the building. If the building is rented, some expense may still be necessary for minor alterations, such as partially removing walls to create larger rooms or increasing the number of toilets in the bathroom. Estimates of cost should be obtained from local contractors. Before getting estimates of costs, health and safety inspections should be made so it is known exactly what additional costs will be necessary. Some additions that may be necessary are fencing around the play yard, floor covering for the classrooms, additional exits, doors that open outward, and protection for windows and stairwells.

Insurance

An insurance agent should be consulted to determine the best insurance coverage for the school. The person consulted should be an independent agent, who would be able to make available the policies of several companies. Responsible adminis-

3. Dorothy B. Boguslawski, *Guide for Establishing and Operating Day Care Centers for Young Children* (New York: Child Welfare League of America, 1968), p. 19.

trators of a school acknowledge insurance to be an essential cost. Some of the kinds of insurance which should be considered are property insurance or tenants' insurance, which covers fire and theft, accident insurance for children, liability for staff, and public liability for any vehicles operated by the school. Often a fidelity bond is obtained for those persons who are responsible for the handling of funds.

Utilities

Heat, light, water, and gas are utilities which will be a part of the expense of every school, except where one or more of these is included in rental for a building. In some cases, an installation fee will be necessary, but these fees should be fairly stable over a period of years, except if rates change or the size of the school changes.

Food

Expenditures for food are minimal in schools which are open for only two or three hour sessions. In an all-day program, a basic amount for food should be allotted and careful records kept to establish a cost per child per meal. The possibility of reimbursement for school lunches and milk under the School Lunch Program should also be investigated. If storage space is available, buying food in quantity in conjunction with another school or agency can result in substantial savings. It it well to check health department regulations regarding the storage of food before purchasing in quantity, paricularly if perishable or frozen food is involved.

Educational Equipment

Equipment means all items which are permanent in the educational program. This includes furniture for the classroom, blocks and other relatively permanent pieces of equipment, toys, books, records, and tricycles. In an initial budget this category represents a considerable expense, as it includes equipment for both indoor and outdoor activities. Although costs will vary considerably, depending on quantity, shipping charges and local resources, budget estimates should include approximately one hundred and ten to one hundred and twenty-five dollars per child for a half-day program.[4] If the program is all day, additional costs will be thirty-five to fifty dollars above the costs of a half-day program to take care of cots, linen, and food service equipment such as dishes and silver, depending on whether these are considered household equipment or educational equipment.

Often costs for equipment can be reduced by having such items as book shelves and toy storage shelves, housekeeping equipment, outdoor climbing apparatus, and possibly tables, constructed locally. Ample money should be allowed in the budget to insure that these items are well constructed and made of the best materials for the purpose, so that they will not need to be replaced for many years. Items used by children need regular cleaning and the finish

4. National Council of State Consultants in Elementary Education, *Education for Children Under Six* (Cheyenne, Wyoming: National Council of State Consultants in Elementary Education, 1968), p. 47.

Courtesy of Educational Facilities Laboratories and George Zimbel

should be able to withstand hard wear. Often repairs cannot be easily made and constant use ruins inferior products.

The equipment purchased with the initial equipment allotment should include as many of the items of basic equipment as possible, as well as large and expensive items which should not soon have to be replaced. If this is done, the yearly budget for replacement of equipment items can be kept to a minimum. It will always be necessary to replenish the supply of such things as dolls, puzzles, books, records, and small toys at regular intervals. For this kind of replacement approximately three to five hundred dollars per group annually should be allowed.

Educational Supplies

The need is constant for the replacement of expendable instructional supplies. Paint, paper, science materials, and clay fall into this category. If the program gives children many opportunities to work with materials, the materials must be there in abundance and in variety. These items should be conserved without causing the children to feel that they cannot have what they need for their projects. The cost of expendable supplies is estimated at two hundred and fifty to three hundred dollars per group annually.[5]

If at all possible, small amounts of petty cash should be available to teachers for the purchase of small items which they could not plan for ahead of time and which they will probably have to buy again. Usually the money spent in this way should be limited, and teachers should know the limits. Accounting for petty cash is difficult, and money spent in this way in a large school could, if permitted, become a sizeable budget item. It is equally undesirable if a teacher must spend her own money for every item she needs for the classroom. For example, if the class is planning to make jello, the teacher should not have to buy the jello, and if the school has a half-day session, it would not be on hand unless ordered in advance by the director with other food supplies.

Household Equipment and Furnishings

All-day programs must have a kitchen fully equipped for the preparation of meals and with adequate sanitary conditions. A

5. *Ibid.*, p. 48.

small half-day program can manage nicely with a small kitchen unit where juice can be refrigerated and where cooking projects can be carried out. A refrigerator is a necessity for all programs to keep food which will be served to the children as snacks.

If the facility has conference rooms, offices, isolation rooms or clinics, furniture must be provided for these. The budget should provide for the purchase of sturdy equipment. Rooms in schools not occupied by a class should be put to multiple uses. Furniture should reflect anticipated uses.

Household Supplies

The chief expenditure for household supplies is for various kinds of paper goods such as toilet tissue, facial tissue, paper napkins, and paper cups. Good record keeping for the first year will provide a sound estimate of the funds needed for these items. For the first year an estimate will be based on the number of children and the amount used during the first few weeks.

Other items include the soaps, cleansers, and other supplies needed for cleaning and sanitation. These must be stored in places to which children do not have access; consequently, the supply which can be purchased at one time may be limited.

Office Supplies

Office supplies needed for a small school are minimal. It may be more economical to have materials duplicated for parents than to employ secretarial help to do them at the school. Most schools do not need much more than the usual desk supplies and school forms.

Publicity

Every school that is just getting started must find some way of informing people of its existence. Newspaper ads and printed posters are two ways that the school can advertise its services. An ad may be placed in the newspaper in the spring, when applications for fall enrollment are being taken. If allowed to run for one or two days, it may be enough to obtain the required number of applicants. Often attractive posters or flyers giving information about the school can be put in places such as grocery stores and laundromats, which are frequented by young parents. If a school is located in a church or community building, publicity can easily be circulated to the membership or to the people using the building for other purposes. In deciding about appropriate publicity, questions must be asked about the program and the people for whom it is intended, as well as the usual avenues that are used for reaching these people.

From time to time, it becomes necessary to advertise positions that are available at the school. The dossiers of prospective teachers may be obtained from the educational placement offices of colleges or universities or by informing other early childhood educators of the vacancy. Prospective aides, cooks, custodians, and maids can be obtained through the U.S. Employment Office or it may be advantageous to run an ad in the help-wanted column of the local paper.

Publicity will have to be given to fund-raising projects. This is usually done through newspaper ads, posters, and radio publicity, if there is a local station with current-events coverage for the community.

The best publicity that a program can have is the recommendation of young parents satisfied with the program. Young parents often take the recommendation of their friends and do not search further for a school for their children.

Postage, Telephone, and Transportation

Time and energy can be saved if the early communication with parents is done by mail. Forms can be mailed out which parents complete and return to the school. The medical form can be mailed early so that the parent has the form when she is ready to take the child to the doctor.

Even more communication will be by telephone. If the school is to maintain close contact with the family, telephone calls must be made back and forth. Budgeting should provide for a business telephone and should include occasional long distance calls. While it is unlikely that the school will make a large number of long distance calls, they may be necessary in connection with the employment of a teacher or with materials ordered from out-of-town companies.

If the school provides transportation for the children to and from school, this must be a budgeted item. Parents might be charged extra for this service, or it might be included in the tuition. Not all schools wish to assume responsibility for transportation. Schools often help parents become acquainted with other parents in the same locality, so that they may organize car pools, or they may refer parents to a company or individual who contracts directly to provide transportation. Charges are then made directly to the parent without the involvement of the school in the arrangements.

Almost all schools have allocated funds for transportation for school trips. For the protection of the children it is usually necessary to use public transportation or to employ a bus or taxi driver who has licensing and insurance. Although most of the trips taken by young children should be in the school's immediate vicinity, a few longer trips will be taken and must be considered in planning the budget.

Professional Development

One way to encourage teachers to attend professional meetings and workshops is to pay for transportation and registration. Money may also be budgeted for tuition in professional courses taken at a university or vocational school. Often professional materials are purchased, such as professional books, magazines, or tapes of speeches that have been delivered at conferences. Money budgeted for this purpose contributes to the long-term development of the staff and school.

Other Services and Goods

An additional budget item is maintenance of equipment. Even the best equipment wears out, and sometimes minor repairs at the proper time can keep it in use for much longer. The amount which should be budgeted for equipment repair is estimated at ten percent of the original cost of the equipment.[6]

A second type of miscellaneous expense is licensing or registration of the program. This expense occurs infrequently and will

6. *Ibid.*, p. 48.

not be very large, unless the services of an attorney are required, as in the case of the school's being incorporated.

PURCHASING MATERIALS

Skillful purchasing and distributing of materials is one way that the administration can contribute creatively to the school's effectiveness and efficiency. The careful selection and purchase of supplies can support the kind of program that is considered best for the children. It is possible to support the creative efforts of staff and to encourage variety and innovation in the program in this way.

Purchasing Practices

Even very small schools require purchasing from a variety of sources. Because of this, it may be very difficult for them to obtain really good buys, unless someone is available to take advantage of bargains when they appear. Even the small school should keep enough cash in its account to permit it to receive discounts on bills. Sometimes vendors will offer a two percent discount if bills are paid within ten days after they are rendered. The amount of cash on hand should also be large enough to allow for purchases of special supplies from auctions or from surplus property stores. Charge accounts should be established only after the vendor has shown that he will provide a range of items required by the school at competitive prices.

Materials and supplies that do not function properly are false economy. Items such as paper towels that do not absorb moisture readily, and paper that cannot be erased without smudges, only frustrate and hinder the staff. They may save money in the original purchase, but in terms of staff time and satisfaction a great deal is lost. If the quality is the same, the school does not usually need to pay for fancy or separate packaging. The storeroom can protect items against damage and keep them clean, if they are stored in boxes or wrapped in plastic.

All major purchases should require the approval of the director of the program. Usually it is better to have one person make major purchases, although if the purchases are for a particular classroom, approval of the staff member who will use them is wise.

Purchasing by too many members of the staff is very expensive in terms of staff time and may cause overexpenditure in some budget categories. Usually it is the director who has full knowledge of the budget allocations and decides whether or not an item can be accommodated within the budget.

Some programs are eligible for tax-exempt status. If this is possible, the school should file a tax-exempt certificate with each vendor with which it has a charge account. Staff members who make cash purchases should also be supplied with a copy of the certificate. Considerable money can be saved over a period of time if the school is tax-exempt.

Purchasing from neighborhood stores is desirable so long as these merchants can meet the school's requirements adequately. It may be that a slight increase in costs is offset by savings in time and transportation. Schools should not feel under obligation, however, to purchase locally when they can benefit from wholesale or quantity prices elsewhere.

Distribution of Supplies and Equipment

A centralized storage space where supplies and equipment are acessible can do much to contribute to the financial management of a school. Centralized storage permits all portable equipment to be cared for and kept in the best possible condition with minimum cost and time. Fewer pieces of portable equipment, such as film projectors and audio-visual machines, are needed if stored in a central location.

Central storage also enables the school to keep inventories more easily and to note when items have to be reordered before the supply is completely exhausted. Necessary measures may be taken to prevent the depletion of certain materials that are badly needed. Items that remain unused on the shelves for exceptionally long periods can be identified. It may be that these materials had been ordered specifically for an upcoming event. It may be that teachers did not know that such materials were available. It could be discovered which items were unsuitable or of inferior quality, or to what possible use they could be put, or how they might be disposed of or resold.

If centralized storage is used, it is very important for the users of the supplies to know that those who make the purchases are sensitive to the needs of the different components of the program so that the practice of hoarding is not established. Large quantities of any kind of supply in one classroom can defeat the purpose of centralized storage, as well as create problems for others who need the materials.

Supplies and equipment should be distributed in a way that is both flexible and business-like. This is simple enough for a school with one or two classrooms, where the personnel work closely together in planning the program. But in large schools and day-care centers, a lot of time could be wasted trying to find out who has what and how long they plan on using it. Equipment that is shared by several classrooms should be checked out for the time it will actually be used. Information on when it will be returned should be part of the reservation procedure so any staff member can tell what equipment is available. Some equipment and supplies will be duplicated, but buying exactly the same equipment for each room is not a good practice when the purchase of similar but different material could enlarge the variety available to any one classroom.

Teachers and other personnel must have access to the storeroom when the program is in session. Some regular procedure for keeping the storeroom open should be worked out. Sometimes it is difficult for storeroom personnel and purchasing personnel to understand that the purpose of equipment and supplies is for the use of the children. It is also sometimes difficult to get teachers to fill out requisitions or make written requests for materials that are needed. Someone should be responsible for reconciling invoices for incoming stock with requisitions for outgoing stock, and the inventory. If this is not done at regular intervals, some materials can disappear and perhaps not be missed until it is too late to do anything about it.

The inventory of equipment should be made each year prior to the school's budget development sessions. This will help to identify what is available for the next year and what amounts need to be budgeted. Budgets cannot be made entirely on the basis of the inventory, as it is necessary to make provision for unforeseen contingencies. It is estimated that a desirable inventory level is one that will carry an organization through two months of operation.[7]

7. Malcolm S. Host and Pearl B. Heller, p. 156.

PAYROLL

Every school has a responsibility to honor scrupulously its obligations to its employees. One of the most important obligations is to pay its employees on time. This is important not only because it is evidence that the management is conscientious about its fiscal affairs but also because it is closely linked to the morale of the staff. How the payroll is managed is a vital administrative tool for making the partnership work between the administration and the staff.

Before selecting the time and length of the pay period, it is wise to investigate local practices. The number of employees who are paid wages, community practices related to rent payment and credit collection, and the cost of living may be factors that affect the length of the pay period. In many areas it is customary to pay those who earn wages rather than salaries every two weeks. In some areas, salaried employees are also paid twice monthly.

Whether employees are paid wages or salaries, they should know the basis used to compute their daily pay rate. Wages are usually based on an hourly rate. In the case of salaries, the daily rate is obtained by dividing the monthly salary by the number of working days in a month. If this information is clear to the employee, misunderstanding and resentment can be prevented when deductions for absences must be made.

Another practice which helps to prevent misunderstanding is to provide the employee with a payroll check which has a stub showing the kinds and amounts of deductions which have been made. Although employees have been told in advance what deductions will be made, it often comes as a surprise when they see how much is deducted from their checks.

Policies regarding vacations and sick leave should be made very clear. An annual statement should be presented to the employee showing how much sick leave and vacation time has accumulated. Policies may vary widely from one school to another. A school that is in session for only nine or ten months does not have to be concerned about vacations other than those which occur during the school year, such as Thanksgiving and Christmas. A school such as a day care center, which operates the year round, must plan to provide vacation time for its employees, which may mean hiring substitutes. There are also policies about the maximum amount of vacation time that may be accumulated, since an organization must eventually pay for vacation time. Employees who resign are entitled to their accumulated vacation time.

Sick leave is viewed somewhat differently from vacation leave. Most schools allow a minimum, ranging from five days per year to one day per month, for sick leave without loss of pay. If employees have used their sick leave judiciously and undergo a lengthy illness, they will often be given special consideration. If sick leave has been used when there was doubt of actual illness, an employee may not be given such consideration. There should be policies that indicate how much sick leave may be accumulated from one year to the next.

Records of hourly employees should be carefully kept. These records need not be any more complex than a regularly kept time sheet showing the time one reports for work, leaves for lunch, and leaves work. There should also be records of overtime, if that is permitted. Policies should be clear on whether employees are to be paid for overtime or given time off instead.

Certain records regarding the payroll are required by law. Annual statements of taxes withheld from each employee's earnings are to be sent to him no later than January 31 of the year following the year in which wages or salaries were paid. W-2 forms, on which this information is to be supplied, are obtained from the Internal Revenue Service. Social Security taxes also require records and quarterly reports which must be filed accurately and on time. The school must deposit the money withheld from salaries in a separate bank account to avoid any suspicion of co-mingling of federal funds with other funds of the school. Co-mingling of federal funds is prohibited by law and violation of this statute carries severe penalties.

Careful records are necessary to administer the payroll responsibly. The school is accountable for all the money that it takes in, and since the payroll makes up a larger portion of this money than any other expense, the greatest care is required in this category.

QUESTIONS FOR DISCUSSION

1. Develop an initial budget for opening a private nursery school which is to be housed in a church at a rental fee of $100 per month. Space available will permit the enrollment of eighteen chil-

dren in the morning and an equal number in the afternoon. A teacher and a paid assistant will comprise the staff. What tuition will the owner need to charge each child per month to meet expenses? How much do you think should be charged to make a fair profit after the program has been in operation for several years, assuming that expenses are roughly the same?

2. Assume that you are the fund-raising chairman for a cooperative nursery school-kindergarten. Discuss the projects you think it would be worthwhile to sponsor. Why do you think these are the most appropriate for the purpose?

3. Develop a statement of sick leave and annual leave policies for a day care center that is in operation all year round. Develop a similar statement for a cooperative nursery school. Compare the two policies.

8 Records and Reports

TEACHERS HAVE VERY DIFFERENT IDEAS ABOUT KEEPING records. In any group of experienced teachers, the topic of record-keeping is likely to evoke controversy. Some teachers see records as an end unto themselves; they do not use the records of other teachers, and they do not see the records they keep as valuable to other teachers. For this type of teacher, record-keeping is another form of red tape, and their records are as routine and minimal as possible.

Others see records as tools to help them meet some of the complex problems of teaching. They are able to handle the mechanics of record-keeping and may be able to offer constructive suggestions to other teachers. A relatively simple record-keeping system, used intelligently, can be an asset to the school and to individual teachers.

WHY KEEP RECORDS?

Gaining Better Understanding of Children

If there is any one universal concern of teachers of young children, it is the desire to know more about individual children in the classroom. In any classroom there are usually one or two children who are particularly perplexing to the teacher. Careful records will often help the teacher determine the specific circumstances under which children are likely to display certain behaviors. If a teacher keeps records of a child's behavior at different times of the day and in different activities, she should be able to identify areas in which the child is confident and competent, and areas in which the child has problems. This background of understanding is essential to any action that the teacher takes to guide the behavior of the child, whether in the area of social development or in curriculum planning.

Helping Parents Understand Children

Parents and teachers often have a very different view of the same child. This may be because the child actually does behave differently at home and at school. Then, too, parents, emotionally involved with their children, often force relatively insignificant behavior or habits to become an issue at home, whereas this behavior never becomes an issue in the classroom. Because parents are so familiar with their children's behavior, they sometimes overlook a disability or a problem. Parents who do not have a wide variety of contacts with children of the same age are not in a position to observe some of the deviations that may be obvious to the teacher. Records of exact episodes which have occurred at school are often convincing to the parent when purely verbal reporting is less effective.

All records used with parents do not have to be those written by the teacher. Parents who observe children's work are quite capable of making some of the same observations about it that teachers make. On the basis of their observations they may ask questions which enable the teacher to give helpful explanations. This may go a long way toward helping the parent improve the kind of understanding and guidance that he or she provides.

Securing Evidence of Growth and Development

Observing the day-by-day changes in children is very difficult for teachers and parents because of their close and continuous involvement with them. Because it is easy for teachers to become involved only with the immediate and most demanding aspects of a child's behavior, it is necessary to keep consistent records over a period of months and years. Close examination of these records can reveal areas in which growth and development is deviating from their established pattern. Knowledge of such changes is particularly important when there are known changes in health, nutrition, family circumstances, or the program of the school.

Discovering and Meeting Special Needs

The special needs of individual children are of great concern to both parents and teachers, and behavior which is indicative of these needs must be accurately described not only for diagnosis but also for prescribing treatment. Often special behavior difficulties and personality needs must be observed and described over a period of time and in a variety of situations. Accurate records take away much of the guesswork and shorten the length of time it takes to acquire the information needed by teachers and specialists to whom the child may be referred. Records kept by a teacher become the basis for referral conferences or for joint conferences with specialists such as psychologists, physicians, nurses, or reading specialists. These records may be essential in helping to place a child in a program which most closely meets his needs, especially if his needs cannot be properly met in the regular classroom.

Providing Data for School Placement

Records of a child's previous school experiences are very important when the child moves from kindergarten into the primary grades. The placement of a child in one class or another may be crucial in determining his adjustment and academic progress. Scores on various reading readiness or development tests, and ratings made by the teacher of his performance in the classroom, often form the basis for the decision. This is particularly important in placing the child who is marginal in his development. In this case, the records often form the basis of a conference with the parents at which the child's progress is discussed and recommendations are made. Particularly when a child's development is not proceeding as rapidly and as smoothly as it should be, teachers should document their observations.

Records are also useful when families must move and enroll their children in nursery schools or kindergartens in a different locality. With the differences in age of entrance and types of programs, records prepared by the child's former school should enable the faculty of the new school to determine the most satisfactory placement for the child. Such records can alert teachers to the kinds of experiences the child previously had and his response to them. They can help the new teacher anticipate the child's behavior and special needs. When older children change schools, records are routinely transferred, but in programs for younger children, records are not always transferred so carefully. One place where these records could be very important is in the transfer from a non-public nursery school or day care center to a public kindergarten, or from a non-public kindergarten to a public school primary program. Schools usually do very little to make records available. Much repetition for the children could be avoided if records were transferred and used.

Serving as Guides for Curriculum Planning

To provide a curriculum to meet the individual needs of children, the teacher must be aware of what the child's needs are—of what he can do and what he cannot do. Some of the child's abilities can be remembered but are likely to escape notice if the teacher does not keep records. These records may consist of check-lists of skills and abilities in relation to the experiences provided. Since many of the abilities emphasized in programs for young children follow a developmental pattern, it is essential for the teacher to know where the child is in the sequence. If the teacher does not know this or does not know how to use the information, the program will not be of maximum value to the child.

Providing In-Service Education for Teachers

One approach in designing an in-service program for teachers is to use their classroom experiences. Classroom records can furnish material for dealing with the complex problems of the teacher and the special problems of individual children. In-service education experiences should be helpful to teachers by introducing new techniques and procedures for teaching. Any time that new techniques are introduced, teachers will need to keep records of what they do and how the children respond. This helps them know whether procedures learned in the in-service program are effective or not.

Providing Data for Research

Many of the records used for research are not kept by teachers. These may be obtained during experimental episodes in which a child is removed from the classroom and taken to an experimental laboratory. Many of the techniques are observational. They may involve one or more observers, and utilize complex systems of coding and recording behavior. Teachers often find that research gives feedback which makes teaching more interesting and stimulating.

RECORDS AND PROGRAM OBJECTIVES

The first step in the development of a record-keeping plan is to develop a clear statement of the objectives of the program. These objectives should cover all aspects of the program and should be stated in behavioral terms setting forth the specific skills the child should develop. The intention is not that all children will attain the same level of competency, but rather to identify the behaviors which the school considers important to provide whatever experiences are necessary for the child to develop his skills. Instead of a fixed standard that all children should reach, what should develop is a continuum along which a child's competency can be located and his progress can be shown. The end result will show children still at different levels of development in relation to the same competency and any individual child's level of development in relation to different competencies.

The records that teachers keep for evaluation will need to show the children's competencies in relation to the specific program objectives. For example, if the teacher wants to know what motor skills a child has, she will plan opportunities for physical activities such as skipping, running, galloping, jumping, etc. She then records her observations, to be used in her planning. Since these are activities that the children will enjoy, the record-keeping involved does not interfere with the children's enjoyment of the activities.

If the teacher wants to know whether children can recognize numerals, she can give them a simple activity with an old telephone or a toy telephone. As the teacher helps the children dial their telephone numbers, she can identify the child who does not know how to locate a numeral. The numerals that are not included in each child's telephone number can just be added as an extra part of the game. Nothing should be said to the children about their relative skills, but the teacher may observe and record information on those who need extra practice in recognizing numerals.

Record keeping in the affective area may not be as simple but is no less important. Information on the child's self-concept can be found in the child's approach to cognitive activities, in his use of his body in physical activities, and in his relationships with other children. Many teachers will need assistance in learning to detect this behavior, which is very important to the child's total learning.

Record keeping, evaluation, and planning become part of a continuous process which the director of a school engages in with the professional staff. If the children are acquiring the competencies which are the objectives of the school, some assumptions can be made about the effectiveness of the program. If the children do not seem to be acquiring these competencies, it becomes necessary to examine the activities that are being provided as opportunities for development. The program may need to be changed, or some of the methods may need to be changed. Evaluation of the program is not an end in itself. Evaluation must always be directed toward remedying weaknesses and recognizing strengths; it should always result in effective change or improvement.

SCOPE OF RECORDS

Records kept by a school fall into several classifications according to the reasons for which they are kept and their degree of permanence. Some records are kept by teachers for their own use. Other records and reports are prepared primarily to be sent to parents. Similar reports, sometimes supplemented by additional materials, may be sent to the child's next teacher. Usually those records which become a part of the permanent file contain the basic information about a child that is essential for placement or in transfer to another school.

General Informational Records

There are certain records that are routinely completed for each child when he enters school, with information about his family background, health information, emergency information, and permission slips. Forms are usually distributed to the parent at registration and are returned when the child enters school.

Family Background. This is usually supplied by the parent and largely consists of factual information about the child's family, such as his parents' names and address, and the number and ages of his brothers and sisters. Sometimes, particularly in the case of cooperative nursery schools, information is requested regarding the family's interests and hobbies that would help the staff best utilize the talents of the parent group.

Much of thc information on the early developmental history of the child is usually requested on this record rather than on the health record, as it is necessary for a parent to supply this information even though it might be requested from the child's physician. A section may be included where the parent indicates the child's relevant experiences or interests. Some records ask parents to report any special problems with the child or any methods of guidance which are particularly effective with him. Such a record is not intended to embarrass a parent or to force him to reveal information he does not want the school to have. It merely allows the school to be aware of such difficulties as extensive health problems, serious behavioral problems, or developmental weaknesses. It is to be hoped that the parent can trust the school not to misuse the information.

Health Record. The importance of physical examinations has been discussed in Chapter Six, so it will be given only a brief mention here. For maximum value, the health examination should be conducted prior to the time the child enters school. If the school is responsible for the health examination, it should be conducted as early as possible during the school year, to provide maximum protection for all the children. These records should be on file for every child and should note any special problems or conditions the child has. This may be confidential information, to be used only by individuals directly concerned with the child.

Emergency Information. Addresses and telephone numbers of parents should be readily available to the teacher or director in case of an emergency. This information should also include the name of the child's physician and the name of a person to be called in case the parent cannot be reached. It can be kept in a small card file near the telephone, where it will be most accessible to the person who is most likely to do the telephoning if a child becomes ill or is hurt.

Permission Slips. Forms should be prepared for each field trip away from the school, indicating to parents where the child will be going, how and when he will be going, and what supervision will be provided. This form should have a place for the parent's signature. Some schools secure a blanket permission, but a permission for each trip is better, since the teacher can then be sure that the parent is aware the child is going. Permission slips do not relieve the school of responsibility for the child while on the trip, but indicate that the child was not taken on the trip without the parent's knowledge, making negligence more difficult to prove.

Records Kept by the Teacher for Her Own Use

Any records kept by the teacher must have a clearly defined purpose to insure that the information kept will be helpful. Earlier portions of this chapter identified some of the purposes records can serve. To assure that records will be maximally useful, teachers must be helped to develop records that are goal oriented and can be used in planning and evaluation. Some of the specific kinds of records which teachers may keep are discussed below.

Anecdotal Records. Most teachers do not question the need for anecdotal records. These provide records of the teacher's daily observations. Anecdotes are particularly helpful to a teacher who is trying to gain additional insight into the behavior of an individual child. They enable her to identify factors in his behavior which could go unnoticed if careful and complete observations were not made, and they enable her to formulate new ways of working with the child. They also allow professionals serving in the role of consultant to the school to have the information they need for discussing the child and raising questions or making suggestions on new approaches the teacher might try.

It is important to focus on the behavior of an individual or group under specific circumstances or in specific situations. Not all behavior recorded should be problem behavior. For example, one of the usual concerns of teachers is how to help children gain acceptance by their peers. Observing the children who seem to have acceptance by large numbers of children and who seem to be able to move with ease from one group to another might help a teacher to discover the behaviors which will need to be taught to the rejected children. Particularly in the area of social behavior, it may be more profitable to study the child who is successful than to focus entirely on the child who has obvious problems.

Teachers usually need a great deal of help in learning to write anecdotal records that are descriptive and unbiased. Some teachers experienced in recording behavior are able to note nonverbal expression—facial expression, movement of hands, feet, or the whole body—as well as verbal expression—conversation and interaction with other children. Teachers also should record and separate inferences from observed behavior. Inferences and interpretations are important, but are of limited value when the teacher cannot distinguish the interpretative data from the objective facts.

Teachers might want to learn easy, inconspicuous ways to carry small cards to note incidents and conversations when they occur. Finding the time to do this in the classroom presents a problem, but if the teacher does it with some regularity, the children will not be distracted and will continue their activities as usual.

Samples of Children's Work. Many teachers find it worthwhile to make a large folder for each child containing samples of the child's work. Paintings can be saved at regular intervals throughout the year, marked with the child's name and date and any pertinent information about the painting. Crayon and chalk drawings, finger paintings, and collages that are not too bulky can also become a part of the folder. The children may help in choosing what is to go into the folder, and in this way be encouraged to leave the work in the folder, instead of taking it home immediately after they are finished. Stories that the child has dictated, or books that he has made, can also become an important part of this file. Unfortunately, much of the work that young children do is so bulky that it is inconvenient to store.

Records of Activities. One way teachers may keep records of children's activities is to use a time-sampling technique involving recording the child's activities at regular intervals during the day. For example, what the child is doing could be recorded at five-minute intervals throughout a day. While not all children could be studied at the same time by this method, several children could be studied, and those studied could be rotated. A much more practical way of sampling what children are doing is to take a few minutes at the end of the work time each morning, or at whatever time the teacher and children can arrange, to write down the various activities a child has engaged in that day. Over a period of weeks and months, the range of a child's activities would be shown. This kind of record helps the teacher determine which areas the children have lost interest in and what materials should be added or temporarily removed.

A teacher who wishes to give more direction to the activities of individual children may utilize a system of cards which record those activities completed by each child for the week. The child would be responsible for reporting what he has done and the teacher could help him plan some of the experiences he should have next. As older kindergarten children become interested in acquiring skills such as writing, this technique allows the teacher to see what progress has been made and what guidance is needed. Such techniques are not usually suitable for children younger than five. Before the teacher and the child engage in any joint planning, children should have the opportunity to choose their own activities. The teacher should also recognize that the objectives of this planning are aimed at helping the child set goals for himself and feel responsible for them. Teachers should guard against assuming too much responsibility for directing the child's activities, as this will tend to make the child dependent on her for deciding what he should do.

Records of activities become very important when the teacher meets with her assistants to plan new experiences for the children and when she has conferences with parents. The larger the number of children in a group, the more important it is to keep this kind of record, as it is possible for the activities of a child to go unobserved for a long time.

Autobiographies. Older preschool children usually like to talk about themselves. This interest can lead to an enjoyable experience when children make books about themselves. This could begin with a photograph taken by the teacher or it might begin with a drawing made by the child. The child would be asked at some time to tell the "Story of Me" which the teacher would write for him or help him dictate to a tape recorder to be transcribed at a later time. This could be a one-time activity or it could be an ongoing activity; the child could add new things from time to time. This may be a very valuable experience in helping to build a bond between the child and the teacher. This is something that the child feels is special to him, and the teacher should reinforce this attitude.

Records Given to the Next Teacher

Any child who has been enrolled in a school for as much as half a year should have a record which can be passed on to his next teacher. These records should give the new teacher information on what experiences the child has had before and how he has responded to them. Information such as attendance, family background, serious illnesses, and accidents might be a part of that record. Facts about the child, such as bilingualism or position in the family, might also be important. Most teachers who come into a classroom at the beginning of a year have to work with the children for a short time before they have an opportunity to talk with their parents. Records can help the new teacher get acquainted with the child until she can obtain her own information.

Although many teachers are very hesitant about passing records along to another teacher and many teachers are just as cautious about using the records of other teachers, any teacher who has had a child in her room for a whole year should have important information about him which could be helpful to his next teacher. If a whole class, or even a small group of children from the same class, is moved along together, the new teacher needs to know what common experiences these children have had. This includes group projects, trips, and particularly any special situations resulting from experiences of various class members, such as foreign travel. In this way the teacher can avoid repeating the same experience for the group during the following year. If the activity is repeated, the teacher will know to begin at a more advanced level than would have been possible during the preceding year.

The second important reason for passing information to the next teacher is to provide information regarding a child's progress. This indicates to the next teacher what the child has been able to do. It should be primarily positive in nature, with emphasis on the various aspects of the child's development. It should provide the new teacher with an idea of the level of the child's functioning when he was last in school. Problem behaviors need not be completely ignored, but they should not be overemphasized or become the major focus of the report. Teachers usually are opposed to passing on information that is too negative or potentially harmful to the child.

Cumulative Records

In every public school there is a permanent record card or folder which is kept on every child from the time he enters school until the time he graduates. These are available if the child ever needs proof of the schools he attended. Often they are used to establish age when other records have been lost or accidentally destroyed.

Cumulative records contain information about the child's date of birth, his parents, the years he was enrolled in the school, testing results, progress reports from year to year, attendance, special awards, and school activities. These records are of necessity kept to the very minimum and are usually composed of factual information about a child, rather than the more personal information that may be kept by the teacher. The cumulative folder may contain material that will be helpful to teachers working with the child but that will not be kept once the child has moved into another school. Some schools object to keeping material in the folder which might reflect negatively on the child. Such material is often removed and placed in a more confidential file if it could hinder the child's school progress in any way.

Reports to Parents

Although conferences with parents are the most common means of reporting to parents in nursery schools and many kindergartens, written reports are sometimes used in kindergartens, particularly in public school kindergartens which have relatively large numbers of children assigned to one teacher and do not provide time for the teacher to have conferences. Use of the written report in kindergarten also tends to correspond with the use of written reports in later grades or class groups of the school.

The report card is one of the least satisfactory ways to report a child's progress. Usually the teacher is forced to report on a child's behavior in broad generalizations which do very little to tell a parent what a child actually does. The report card may also include information on insignificant behavior, such as tying shoes or following directions, which tends to distort the actual purpose of the kindergarten program. When report cards of this sort are used they may cause the teacher to emphasize the behaviors which will be reported to the parents. Some reports which are essentially check lists provide a place for the teacher and parents to add comments. If well used, this is probably the most useful part of the report card.

Narrative reports are much more difficult to write and pose an almost impossible task for a teacher who is responsible for more than twenty children. Such reports, however, can provide the parent with information regarding the experiences the child has been having and how the child has responded. The satisfactory writing of this kind of report is strongly dependent on the records of individual children that have been kept by the teacher, and the ability of the teacher to write descriptively and sensitively about the child. The teacher must know the child well and must be able to separate opinion from actual fact about what the child is able to do. Broad interpretations of the child's behavior tend to make this kind of record meaningless and subject to ridicule. Teachers who can write these records well and who are willing to take the time to do it often receive very favorable responses from parents. The parents are appreciative when they feel the teacher shows real insight into the child's behavior. Parents, too, are well acquainted with their children and recognize when the individuality of the child appears in the report, even though not all of what is reported is entirely positive.

POLICIES ON RECORDS

Policies for the use of records must be developed with the intention of protecting children on whom the records are kept. Such policies may dictate that some records be quite accessible to all the staff and others available to teachers only upon request. Some records may need to be interpreted by the psychologist or physician affiliated with the school. Much will depend on the sophistication of the staff and their ability to use records constructively.

Professional use of records dictates that their content not be discussed with other teachers or aides, except when the discussions are a part of professional conferences. Often a chance remark to a parent leads to additional questions, and before long information which should be kept confidential has become known to several people. One of the first professional lessons a teacher should learn is use of good judgment regarding sensitive information about children.

A second aspect of the professional use of records concerns the way the teacher responds to the information she is given. The teacher should objectively consider any information she has about a child before making any professional decisions. Whether the information is negative or positive, she can consider it in light of other information, and she can use it without being influenced for or against the child. Children are known to behave differently in different classrooms at least part of the time. If the teacher knows something of the child's past history, she may be able to take preventive steps so that the particular situation which provokes certain negative behavior may never develop. She may be able to stimulate children because she knows what they respond to, rather than having to find out by trial and error. To do this, the teacher must be in control of her emotions and respond on a professional level rather than an emotional one.

Central to the issue of how records are used professionally is the issue of when teachers should read records. Some teachers argue that reading records before they have become familiar with the children for themselves will cause prejudice against certain children. Others maintain that if the teacher reads the records before the child comes into class, she will be better prepared to deal with the child when he enters the classroom. Some teachers think records should be referred to only when problems develop. None of these attitudes is completely justifiable. It seems desirable for teachers to become familiar with children and their records at the same time. Records will need to be examined throughout the year, with reference to specific information that might have had no significance at the beginning of the year. Perhaps a good suggestion would be to have the teacher review the records just after she makes her first report. In this way she could function independently of the record yet use it in her work with the child.

QUESTIONS FOR DISCUSSION

1. Devise a record-keeping system for a day care center that is just being organized. Which of the records do you think are most important? Why?

2. How do you feel about keeping and using records? How do you account for your feelings about this particular aspect of teaching?

3. Collect several forms used to gather background information about kindergarten children. Which questions on the forms do you consider appropriate? Which ones do you think should not be asked?

4. What do you consider the particular problems of the cooperative nursery school in the use of records? What records might a cooperative nursery school have that a public school kindergarten might not have?

5. Talk to two teachers about how they feel about the use of records. Report these conversations, pointing up the differences in the views expressed by the teachers.

9 Parent and Community Involvement

UNLIKE SCHOOLS FOR OLDER CHILDREN, EARLY CHILDHOOD programs often rely heavily on the involvement of parents to provide for a quality program. Part of this arises from the early history of early childhood programs, which placed almost as much emphasis on the education of mothers as it did on the education of young children. Contrary to critics of early childhood education who argue that schools will replace the home in the rearing of the child, nursery schools and kindergartens have often been created by the parents whose children they were designed to serve. Parents have definite ideas regarding what experience they want for their children, and many of them are willing to invest considerable effort in achieving what they want.

A POINT OF VIEW ON INVOLVEMENT

In this country we believe that parents have the right to rear their children as they see fit. In actual practice, the right of the parent to bring his child up as he chooses is abridged in a number of ways to insure the safety and education of the child. Most states legislate compulsory education. Every parent must send his child to school during certain years of the child's life. This requirement grows as much out of the cultural need to maintain the social order as from the personal needs of children and their parents.[1]

In the case of early childhood programs, parents make the decision whether to enroll a child and whether to keep him there,

1. Bernard Spodek, *Teaching in the Early Years* (Englewood Cliffs, N.J.: Prentice-Hall, Inc., 1972), p. 257.

Courtesy of Educational Facilities Laboratories and George Zimbel

since education is not compulsory until the child is six or seven. How the parent feels about the program and the teacher is of vital importance to the parent, the school and the child. Both the teacher and the parent have a responsibility for what happens to the child, and neither can work completely independently of the other. The most desirable program for the child results only if a cooperative working relationship is established.

Involvement in Relation to Parents' Goals

Teachers often need to be reminded that they do not "own" the child, that while they have a certain expertise and insight that parents may not have, they do not have an inalienable right to set all the goals and make all the decisions regarding any child's education.

Most young parents who enroll their children in early childhood education programs do so because they believe the school has something to offer the child and the family. They don't usually want to move in and make over the program, but they do have ideas they would like to express. They wish to feel that their ideas are important enough to be listened to and considered, along with the ideas of other parents. What the child learns at home and what he learns at school overlap tremendously in the nursery school years. The parent and the teacher are in a better position than they ever will be again to know the child as the same child.

The issue, then, is the extent to which parents' wishes and demands should constitute a legitimate set of restraints upon the actions of teachers. Traditionally, many schools have kept parents out of decision-making roles except at the very broadest level. Currently, however, the change is being made towards more involvement by parents and other community members in important areas of decision-making, such as school policy and classroom practice.

The distinction between policy-making and practice is not always easy to make. Parent involvement in policy making seems to be legitimate. Setting goals seems to be a procedure in which parents should be involved, in which their ideas should be respected and taken into account by teachers when they are planning classroom activities.

Parent involvement in classroom practice is slightly different. If parents who have no special training in teaching young children are to be the determiners of practice, the need for a qualified teacher no longer exists. A parent may be quite clear about what he wants for his child, but he may be entirely lacking in knowledge of the most desirable techniques for attaining these goals. In this respect he must look to the teacher for leadership. The teacher who has had special training in the developmental characteristics of children and in curriculum planning and classroom techniques is in a much better position to help the child in the classroom than the majority of parents. This is something which parents usually recognize.

Not all parents wish to be involved in their children's

education in the same way or to the same degree. Respecting this difference among parents also poses a problem. Does one assume that all parents want to be involved in their childrens' education, or does one accept the fact that some really do not care about their childrens' education and actually do not want to be involved? This is not an easy question to answer. Probably it helps to assume that some parents are ready to be involved and some are not. It also helps to assume that a parent who rejects one kind of involvement may seek some other kind of involvement. If these assumptions are true, involvement is a very individual matter and parents must be relied upon to make their own decisions regarding how they will contribute. Satisfying involvement on the part of some parents may awaken the interest of other parents.

Involvement Is Gradual

Like any other activity, individual involvement in the activities of the school requires, at the least, a certain amount of interest and willingness to learn the required skills. No one is more aware of his limitations than a parent who has a child in school for the first time. He must learn the skills which enable him to make a contribution, and he must be willing to give the time required to perform the job well. Parents are very different in this respect. Some parents are trained in leadership skills and make very effective leaders of adult groups. Some are trained as teachers and could perform classroom activities as well as the teacher. Others have married right out of high school and have little or no professional training. These factors make a difference in the willingness and abilities of parents to enter into school activities.

Usually parent leadership evolves gradually. Parents are asked by other parents or school authorities to serve in various ways. In this way they get to be known, and their responsibilities are increased. Gradually, as other parents move out of the school because their children enter different programs, new groups move into leadership positions. Some parents unwilling to be involved the first year will accept some responsibility the second year a child is in school or will share a responsibility with another parent with whom they feel comfortable.

Recognition Is Essential

Any parent who is involved in a program should share in the satisfaction of having it work out well. All roles which parents take must be appreciated. This appreciation may come from the teacher or from another parent. If the children are recipients of the service, their response may be the reward of the person who contributes to the program. It is the responsibility of the school director to see that every contribution is recognized. To a certain extent this recognition is an attitude established within the school and helps teachers and children do little things to show their appreciation, such as verbal "thank you's," notes or telephone calls to an individual, or sharing children's remarks with the parent.

ATTITUDES AFFECTING INVOLVEMENT

Every teacher or parent brings his own background of experience to the early childhood program. For one person, school may have been a most enjoyable experience; for others, the school experience may have been devastating. Whatever these experiences were, they will influence how parents and teachers react to school.

Parent Attitudes

Every parent has a different set of attitudes towards school. One mother may be uncertain of her role as a parent. Another mother may feel that her child is outstanding in all ways and that his behavior is perfect. Another mother may know her child has problems; she may not be able to set any limits for the child, and he may be lacking in self-control. Some mothers will send their children to school to get rid of them for a few hours a day. Other mothers may feel that they are growing older and are no longer needed by their children to the extent that they were needed when the children were infants.

In view of these feelings, one potential source of tension between the mother and the teacher is a subtle competition between the teacher and the mother for the child's affection. Nursery school, or even kindergarten, is often the first occasion for separation of the parents from their young child. While separation is often viewed as a problem for the child, there is a complementary stress for the mother.

She may feel that she has been rejected by the child, particularly if the child is very happy at school and seems to prefer school to home. He may also make frequent references to the teacher and what she does, in such a way that it causes the parent to feel inadequate. Although such feelings may not be within the awareness level of the parent, they may still influence the way the parent responds to the teacher.

Some parents see the teacher as a potential evaluator and critic. Parents may feel that they are responsible for the child's behavior, whether it be "good" or "bad," and that the teacher will blame them for how the child behaves. These parents, although they do not often express this doubt, are afraid that the teacher will find something about their children which indicates parental failure to do an adequate job. Even a very tactful teacher may have difficulty discussing the behavior of this parent's child.

Mothers also worry about the normalcy of their children. In some cases, this is an unwarranted concern. In other instances, however, there have been illnesses or other physical or emotional factors which have given the parent legitimate reason for concern. How the mother feels about her child in this respect may have a great impact on how she treats the child and what she encourages him to do. If she feels that her child is very bright, the experiences that she provides for him may be quite different from those provided for a child suspected of being slow. In the latter case, lack of stimulation may be so great as to have a negative effect on the child's development. Some parents are so anxious they can not accept the child's abilities for what they are and provide the right amount of stimulation to help the child grow and develop in his own way.

The parent's own school experiences are a constantly interfering factor. Over the years of school attendance every parent has developed a view of teachers. In his experience teachers may have been authoritarian, or they may have been understanding and helpful. They may have been fair and encouraging, or they may have been sarcastic and punitive. The parent may have been a successful student, or one who almost never experienced success. Though most parents want to do whatever they can to help their children, sometimes their early school experiences may be a handicap, and make it literally impossible for them to feel secure and comfortable in their relationships with teachers.

Attitudes of Teachers

Because they are "people" with some of the foibles which affect people, teachers, too, sometimes have feelings and attitudes which interfere with their relationships with parents. How the teacher feels about the mother's interest in her child can make a difference in her reaction to both the child and the parent. Difficulty may arise if the teacher feels the mother is disinterested in her child. The teacher may also feel that the mother has neglected or mistreated her child. One of the most interfering attitudes is the teacher's idea of what a child "should" be like. Because of prior experiences with his brother or sister of the same family, the teacher may have formed a stereotype of what the child should be able to do or how he will act. Such a stereotype could be either negative or positive, but in either case it does not allow for the real behavior of the child. A teacher who has this attitude has difficulty presenting a child to his parent as he really is. The difficulty is particularly great if the teacher's stereotype of the child differs from that held by the parent.

An attitude which is particularly difficult for some teachers to deal with is the feeling that the mother pushes the child. Many teachers of young children feel that "pushing" young children is a most undesirable thing for parents to do. They feel that such parents are unfeeling in their expectations for the children and that to some extent they are denying the child's right to be young. General misunderstanding is likely to result, with the teacher feeling that the parent pushes too much and the parent feeling that the teacher does not provide a stimulating program for the child.

Disparity of cultural backgrounds is another area which contributes to difficulty in communication. The extent to which the family and the school share similar goals, expectations, and patterns of achievement is particularly relevant when children come from low-income families and teachers come from middle-class backgrounds. One of the characteristic attitudes of teachers toward low-income families is that they do not care about their children, an attitude which has been shown by Head Start to be untrue. On the contrary, many of these parents see school as the beginnings of opportunity for their children, and view success in school as one of the most important things their children can accomplish. Fortunately, today many teachers are becoming more aware of the effect of cultural differences and are beginning to change their attitudes.

Many good teachers do not have any of these attitudes, and many teachers communicate well with parents. They are able to accept a parent as he is, as well as accept his child. Parents are not a threat to all teachers, just as teachers are not a threat to all parents.

PARENT EDUCATION

Parent education is not new. It has been a part of the program of the National Congress of Parents and Teachers for many years. Cooperative nursery schools, in particular, have often devised elaborate programs of parent education. What is new is the attempt to apply research techniques to discover what is accomplished through the varied parent education programs.

Several strategies have been used to promote parent involvement in the education of their children. Sometimes these have been used in addition to provision for a school program for the children. Sometimes the major purpose was to help the parents supply the educational experience. Some programs have been quite carefully evaluated to find out what is actually being accomplished. Enough information is accumulated so that it is possible to speculate on the potential benefits to be derived from parent education.

Strategies of Parent Education Programs

In a study of various programs of parent involvement, Tudor[2] identified home visits, classroom observation and participation, and group meetings as the three basic strategies used to promote parental involvement in the educational process. Programs did

2. Kay Tudor, *Parent Education Today,* Unpublished paper prepared at Indiana University, 1972, 23 pp.

not concentrate on one particular strategy, but instead utilized a combination of strategies.

Home Visits The most common strategy used to promote parent involvement is the home visit. Experiences that occur during the home visit are unique to each program.

The parent education program employed by Karnes[3] consisted of weekly two hour meetings during which the mothers of disadvantaged infants between the ages of twelve and twenty-four months learned the "teaching principles" for various educational toys to be used in the home. The weekly meetings included a child-centered activity such as presentation of toys and materials with an appropriate teaching model, and a mother-centered activity such as a group discussion of discipline techniques. The home visit was made monthly by a paraprofessional to reinforce the teaching principles acquired at the meetings. Thus, the child's tutor became the mother, who was encouraged to work with the child at home.

A similar program was conducted by Gordon,[4] in which the parent educators were also paraprofessional. Instruction of the mothers occurred on a weekly basis in the home of the child. Materials and stimulation exercises were presented to the mother to promote learning by imitation. Mothers received instruction in the importance of play, and in ways to stimulate and amuse the child. Part of the training program included teaching the mothers to make simple toys and mobiles from inexpensive household objects. Issues of *Life* and *Ebony* were taken to each home for the families to enjoy and later utilize in exercises that made use of magazine pictures in labeling and identification.

In the DARCEE program at George Peabody College, mothers from the community were trained to take on the duties of the "home visitor." The home visit was used to supplement the Head Start and/or first grade curriculum, or as the only intervention technique. The mothers received instruction in cognitive tasks

3. Merle B. Karnes et al., *An Approach for Working with Mothers of Disadvantaged Children: A Pilot Project* (Urbana, Illinois: ERIC Microfiche No. ED 017 335 no date), pp. 1–30.

4. Ira Gordon, *Early Stimulation Through Parent Education: Final Report* (Gainesville, Florida: University of Florida, ERIC Microfiche, No. ED 033 912, 1969), pp. 1–233.

or physical training, and were left to work with their child during the remainder of the week.[5]

The Ypsilanti Home Teaching Project[6] was an effort to explore the feasibility of sending teachers into the homes of disadvantaged families to provide a training program for the mother and a tutoring program for the pre-school child without an accompanying classroom program. Each mother and four-year-old child were visited for one and one-half hours per week and were involved in a carefully individualized program. The contact was to permit the systematic development of the foundations necessary for the intellectual functioning of the child through direct tutoring of the child by the teacher. It also provided for the development of language, teaching, and child management skills in the mother through direct mother-teacher interaction during the tutoring session.

Television programs designed by the Appalachia Educational Laboratory were used in conjunction with the home visit strategy to reach many disadvantaged children to whom schools were not accessible. The television programs were designed for children from three to five years old, and were presented each day for a period of thirty minutes. A trained paraprofessional also made a weekly visit to confer with the parents, and to give them instructional materials. In addition, group instruction was provided once each week, through the use of a mobile classroom conveniently set up near the home of the parents and small children.[7]

These programs, all moderately successful in improving the parent's effectiveness, are examples of the range of the home visit strategy. There are numerous other programs, some similar to and some differing from those described.

Classroom Observation and Participation. Although classroom observation and participation have been used for a num-

5. Susan W. Gray and R. A. Klaus, "The Early Training Project: A Seventh Year Report," *Child Development*, 41 (1970): 909–924.
6. David Weikart and Dolores Z. Lambie, "Preschool Intervention Through a Home Teaching Program," in *Disadvantaged Child*, ed. Jerome Hellmuth (New York: Brunner/Maxel, 1968), Vol. 2, pp. 435–500.
7. *Evaluation Report: Early Childhood Education Program, 1969 Field Test, Appalachia Educational Laboratory* (Charleston, West Virginia: ERIC Microfiche, No. ED 041 626, 1970), pp. 1–204.

ber of years in the education of parents, little has been written about these projects, and little evaluation has been made. One cooperative nursery school, the Juniper Gardens Parent Cooperative Nursery School,[8] has described its program. The mothers in this cooperative school participated actively in the classroom while undergoing a parent training program which consisted of a tutorial and group activities which taught the mother techniques of classroom management. The tutorial was a series of individual lessons designed to teach pre-academic concepts and skills.

One program of Parent-Child Educational Centers,[9] conducted by Arizona State University, involved parents in the planning and carrying out of the activities in the center. This program, unlike most programs, stipulated that both fathers and mothers had to participate in the program.

Programs involving parents in classroom observation and participation are usually planned to achieve at least two objectives: to help parents develop a better understanding of the behavior of preschool children, specifically their own preschool child, and to help them to develop an understanding of the curriculum and procedures for guiding preschool children. Such programs, while focusing on the observation of children in groups, are usually directed towards helping the parent improve his skills in guiding his own child in the home situation.

Group Meetings Almost every educational program for young children provides some group meetings to serve as a means of interpreting the school program to the parents. Often parent participation consists largely of attending meetings and asking occasional questions. Some programs have been a bit more enterprising and have expanded the content of the meetings to include areas of child development, nutrition, discipline, language development, and other topics of current interest. They have also planned these meetings to take various forms, such as lectures, small group discussions, and activity-oriented workshops.

8. *The Juniper Gardens Parent Cooperative Nursery: Final Progress Report* (Kansas City, Missouri: ERIC Microfiche No. ED 032 920, 1968), pp. 1–38.
9. H. E. Moore and I. W. Stout, *A Plan of Action for Parent-Child Educational Centers* (Arizona State University, Tempe, Arizona: ERIC Microfiche No. ED 027 959, 1968), pp. 1–30.

Although group meetings do not usually provide for as much personal involvement and commitment on the part of parents as the two strategies previously discussed, one approach developed by Glenn Nimnicht at the Far West Laboratory for Educational Research and Development[10] provides a very innovative approach to the group meeting. The program consists of a parent-child course accompanied by access to a "toy library." The program is designed for parents of three or four-year-olds to help them help their children develop a positive self-image and intellectual skills, and to improve parent-child interaction. The course meets for two hours weekly, during an eight-week period. Discussion of the use of specific educational toys and their accompanying "learning episode" takes place during the weekly session. The toys and learning episodes are then taken home for the following week, used in the home, evaluated by the mother, and returned to the library.

Evaluating Parent Education Programs

Measuring the effects of a parent education program is very complex, because of the many variables that the experimenter is not able to control and because of the difficulty of isolating the specific effects of one strategy.

The most consistently positive results of parent education programs are in the area of attitudinal changes on the part of participating parents, and/or increased interest in their children and the educational process.[11] One study in particular, *The Nurseries in Cross-Cultural Education,* attempted to bring together various races and various social classes in the program. The staff who conducted the home visits program found that the mothers became more at ease in the school environment and became more objective in observing their child's growth and progress. The parents were observed to be more adaptable, open, and accepting of other parents who were different from themselves. They developed an acceptance

10. Glenn Nimnicht, *A Progress Report on the Parent-Child Course and Toy Library* (Berkeley, California: Far West Laboratory for Educational Research and Development, ERIC Microfiche No. ED 045 206, 1970), pp. 1–34.
11. Tudor, p. 16.

of each other within the group, regardless of race or social class.[12]

Research generally confirms the correlation between parent participation and positive effects on the child's cognitive development and language skills, as well as on the parent's child-rearing practices and the quality of parent-child interaction. Some studies do not show any positive effects on the child or the parent, but no research has been conducted which indicates that parent education is detrimental to the development of the child or his relationship to his parents. In order for a parent education program to produce maximum effects, it must use a holistic approach in dealing with the families. Evidence suggests that parent education, as it was conducted, did not really meet the needs of the parents, and that parents needed help in solving their own overwhelming problems before they could possibly be expected to focus on the child and his education.[13]

One of the important questions still left unanswered is whether parents want to be educated. Another is what constitutes the most significant content of parent education, and for what groups of parents? For example, is parent education for middle-class parents different from parent education for low-income parents? Is the content's relevance to the parents' needs and interests more important than its uniformity with what professionals might consider significant? We still have a long way to go, as research findings in this area are insufficient.

INVOLVING PARENTS

While parent education is a very desirable kind of parent involvement, it may or may not be directly related to the educational program that the child is experiencing. Ways need to be found to provide direct communication between the parents and the administration and teachers in the program. This can be done through parent participation in advisory committees, through parent

12. Mary B. Lane et al., *Nurseries in Cross-Cultural Education, Final Report* (San Francisco State College, School of Education: PHS Grant No. A11 MHO 1976 and Rol MH 14782, 1971), pp. 1–463.
13. Tudor, p. 16–19.

participation in classroom activities and if possible through direct face-to-face contacts between the parent and the teacher.

Advisory Committees and Governing Boards

Many early childhood programs have a governing board or an advisory committee. The persons who make up such boards should be citizens interested in the services that the school provides and should be willing to give some time to making decisions that are important to the program. Board members should be sought in accordance with the purposes of the program, so that they supply the expertise needed to make the necessary decisions regarding the program. For some programs, board members should be chosen from various sectors of the community: from many ethnic and religious groups, from various political groups, and from the ranks of professional and nonprofessional workers. Most important, it is essential that parents of children served by the program be represented on the board.

Governing boards of most schools make a practice of establishing a number of standing committees. These committees are valuable because when the governing board is small, they help to distribute the workload and involve considerably more people. Such committees constitute a very important way of involving parents. Committee participation not only encourages them to contribute but also helps to keep them informed about the important decisions that are being made. In the cooperative nursery school and in the day care center, these committees do much of the work and make many of the recommendations that are eventually acted upon by the governing board.

Working with governing boards and committees takes much of the director's time and energy. A satisfactory relationship grows out of a series of encounters in which the director demonstrates that she can be trusted and that she has an honest concern for the children in the program. Ultimately the role of the director in working with a board is to help in the making of decisions. Sometimes it is difficult for the director to accept decisions that are different from those she would make. She must try to insure that parents have appropriate information upon which to base their decisions. The director can also help the board anticipate how its decisions will affect the program and the people involved. She should be able to work with a board so that they move independently and responsibly. The ability of the director to work with parents in the development of long-range plans and basic policy requires personal qualities and professional competencies.

Parent Participation in the Classroom

Parent participation in the classroom became recognized as an essential part of the program of a cooperative nursery school because of the benefits provided to both the school and the parents. It has since become such an intergal part of programs like Head Start and Follow Through that many public schools now use parent volunteers as teacher aides in the classrooms.

There are many ways that parents may participate in classrooms. In some programs the participation is on a regularly scheduled basis, with the parent acting as an assistant teacher and helping children in many informal ways. In other programs parents may participate only at designated times, when they have been asked to help with special projects. Parents with special talents in music, dancing, and art are usually in demand and may take a leadership role in these activities when they are there. Some schools invite parents to help only with parties, trips and similar occasions. This is helpful to the teacher, but the special nature of the occasion may give the parent an unrealistic view of usual classroom activities.

When parents are regular participants in the classroom, an orientation program should be planned to provide them with help in acquiring the skills they will need in working with the children. These parents need to know about the program, including the daily schedule of activities and the behavior which is expected of the children. If there are special routines or special instructions for the use of any particular piece of equipment, these should be presented verbally, and also given to the parents in written form. Each time the parents arrive, they should be told their specific responsibilities and any other information relevant to the day's activities. Time should be planned at the end of the day to discuss problems, answer questions, and evaluate what happened during the session.

Handbooks prepared for parent participants are very helpful. These, however, are not sufficient without some additional explanation and instruction from the teacher. Parents may even work with the teacher to develop such a handbook, since parents are apt to know what kind of information other parents want. The teacher may want to do the final version of the handbook, but parent contribution to the book will increase its usefulness.

Working with parent participants sometimes takes unusual patience on the part of the teacher, when the parent's methods of working with the children are quite different from the techniques employed in the school. Little differences in ways of handling children can often be overlooked when no serious difficulty seems to result, but a teacher may sometimes have to point out to a parent that his or her behavior is creating a problem. The parents' good will is more important than minor inconsistencies in dealing with the children.

Parent Interviews

The parent interview is one of the most worthwhile contacts between teachers and parents. Here, in a face-to-face situation, the people most concerned about a child can share their observations of his behavior and plan effective ways of guiding him.

Parent interviews are used less often than they might be because they are very time-consuming. Yet parents and teachers usually find that the time is well spent in terms of the quality of the resulting relationships. Sometimes it is possible to reduce the length of parent interviews by discussion of some common problems and questions in meetings of small groups of parents.

Parent interviews are most successful if they are planned at regular times during the year. Additional interviews can be initiated at other times by either the teacher or the parent. Usually the first interview should be held early in the year. Some teachers like to hold this interview a few days before the opening of school, so that they can meet each parent individually. Other teachers feel that it is better to hold the first interview during the first weeks of school, after they have become familiar with the child.

This interview held at the beginning of the year provides an opportunity for the teacher to become acquainted with the family. The parent has an opportunity to talk about the child's favorite activities, playmates, and toys. The really delightful characteristics of the child can be discussed. Since most parents enjoy talking about their children, this kind of interview helps them develop a friendly relationship with the teacher. During the interview, the teacher may also give the parent some information about the program and explain any special materials the child may need.

As the school year progresses, additional interviews should be held. The time that the interviews are held indicates the kind of information that is exchanged. At mid-year the parent will continue to share information about the child's activities at home, his likes and dislikes, his feelings, his interests and especially any school-related problems. The teacher can describe how the child interacts with other children and adults, how he participates in the various aspects of the school program, and how his behavior reveals changes in his skills, attitudes and ideas. The teacher may also talk about the program and the reasons for having some activities, in relation to the needs of the children. Through this kind of exchange, the teacher and parents develop an excellent basis for planning the child's continuing development.

A conference held at the end of the year will focus more on the child's behavior at school, with special emphasis on the changes which have occurred during the year. The parent will of course contribute by sharing his observations, but the emphasis will shift towards the teacher's observations. This is an appropriate time to discuss experiences that might be worthwhile for the child during the summer, or to discuss any techniques which have been used either successfully or unsuccessfully with the child. Whatever questions the parent has should be discussed thoroughly and honestly.

Occasions will arise during the year when either the parent or the teacher will want to initiate a conference. Special behavior problems occurring either at home or at school, the child's not wanting to go to school, unusual family happenings that the teacher needs to be informed about, extended absences, or constant late arrival, might be helped by a conference between the parent and the teacher.

School Visits

School visiting as it is discussed here is more of an occasional occurrence than a regularly-scheduled activity. When an extensive program of parent education is not carried out, visits are very important in helping the parent understand some of the activities of the class.

If visiting is to become a very worthwhile part of the program, some planning must be done for it. Fathers, for example, have a very hard time visiting school during regular times, so it might be wise to plan a short session at a time convenient for fathers. It is also helpful to plan care for younger siblings to make it possible for a mother to visit who could not otherwise arrange to come. As mothers become acquainted with each other, they might agree to take turns caring for children too young to visit. Although younger preschool children are not usually permitted to visit without the mother, one younger child could visit with a mother without causing any disruption. On a special occasion such as a birthday, a parent might be encouraged to take time off from work to be with her child. Talking with a parent will often reveal what might be done to make a visit easy.

Informal Contacts

Informal contacts should not take the place of planned involvement with parents, yet the informal communication between parents and teachers does much to further good relationships. Frequently, teachers and mothers see each other in the morning when the child arrives and in the late afternoon when he leaves for home. This is no time to discuss an involved problem, but the little exchanges of information in one or two sentences can be very worthwhile to both. Usually such exchanges should be factual in nature, since the child is present. The child may even be the bearer of news that is helpful to the teacher, and he may be encouraged to do most of the talking, with a few added comments by the parent.

In some communities, the parents will invite a child's teacher to lunch or for a visit after school. Such occasions are usually enjoyable and enable the teacher and child to see each other in a different setting.

Community events may also afford informal contacts with children and families. Schools and teachers who wish to promote such activities might plan family picnics or covered-dish dinners to which the children can invite brothers and sisters as well as parents. A few such activities can sometimes do wonders to promote a warm feeling towards the school. If there is a variety of informal contacts, various families may be reached in different ways, since not all will respond positively to just one activity.

It only takes a few minutes of a teacher's time to write a short personal note to a parent to show appreciation or to report an important event for the child. Teachers who don't like to write notes might pick up the phone and make a short call. This kind of communication is much more effective for reporting positive incidents than for discussing problems. It is a way the teacher can communicate to a parent that she cares, which sometimes is more important than the actual message. Problems call for an interview, as written messages are easily misunderstood. Telephone conversations need to be kept short and should not require that the parent talk about the child, as the teacher does not know how much privacy the parent has.

TRAINING PROGRAMS FOR STAFF

Training programs should be provided for staff so that they will work toward common goals in their curriculum planning and so that the experiences provided by the school will have continuity and depth without unnecessary repetition. Such programs, if well conducted, can help to create a cohesiveness and an attitude which says to the parents and the community: "This is our program; we are proud of our school." The next step is to spread this cohesiveness to the parents.

Just as teachers have different ideas about curriculum, they also have different ideas about working with parents. Certainly no training program should destroy the individuality of the teacher in her work with parents. Yet without some general agreement on goals of the school for working with the parents, teachers could go in quite different directions and present a confusing image of the school.

Regular staff meetings provide one avenue that can be used to develop the program. Here the staff can share information about special happenings, draw on their knowledge of each child and each family, and talk about what they are trying to achieve in their individual classrooms. Here they can meet on an equal basis and learn from one another, whether the persons involved are teachers, family workers, or the director of the school. From time to time, parents may be invited to the meetings, particularly parents who are in leadership positions such as chairman of the board, chairman of the class representatives, or special committee chairmen. Each staff member has a contribution to make. Sometimes it is knowledge of a child or a parent, or special insight into a community problem. This special knowledge can come out as practical problems are discussed. Each member of the staff must feel comfortable in expressing what he knows and thinks, and must not feel that his contribution is less important than that of other staff members.

Seminars led by the director, the coordinator of parent activities, or an outside resource person may be set up to give teachers more intensive help in working with parents in the classroom. Such sessions could help teachers become aware of parents' concerns in general, learn to encourage parents who participate in the classroom as aides to the teacher, and develop discussion techniques to use in group meetings with parents. Content can be varied as the needs of the teachers change and as they become more skilled in some areas. Often informal reports of classroom activities can be used as the basis for discussion. Resource people can be used occasionally in connection with the staff meetings and seminars, when particular expertise is needed.

INDIVIDUAL CONTACTS WITH PARENTS

Creating an atmosphere where teachers and parents can talk, and where parents feel welcome, requires a minimum of effort on the part of the teacher. It would seem that it might not be necessary to make such suggestions to teachers as "Greet the parents by name and engage them in friendly conversation." Yet not all teachers engage in informal contacts like these, and do not realize how important they can be in building a positive learning situation. Usually there are events of a pleasant nature which have occurred at school, or there are events in the family that the teacher can inquire about, such as the child's new pet or the trip taken to grandmother's house.

Interviews with parents should be planned so that they will not be interrupted. They must be scheduled with ample time, so that the next parent will not arrive before the interview is finished. Another adult should be around, just in case the child or a younger sibling is brought along. Precautions should be taken so that another teacher or colleague will know that the interview is in session and will not take this time to borrow a piece of equipment or a felt pen.

Whatever the teacher says to the parent should be truthful and honest. Parents must feel that when they ask a teacher a question they get an honest answer. The actual reply may be that the teacher does not know, but parents will respect an honest answer more than they will respect an attempt to sugar-coat, flatter, or mislead. The teacher should be as tactful as possible, giving the parent as much objective information as is possible.

Often informal conversation at the beginning of a conference helps the teacher find out how the parent feels about the child. This can give the teacher some clues on how the parent feels about behavior that the teacher may wish to discuss, so she can help the parent see the child's behavior more realistically, if this is needed. Sometimes it is not easy for a teacher to realize just how sensitive a parent is about his child, especially when the child's behavior may seem to the parent to reflect on his ability as a parent. It may mean that certain aspects of the child's behavior are not discussed at the first conference unless the parent seems to want to pursue them. The teacher may feel that the area is too sensitive and had better wait until a later date.

Often teachers are asked direct questions about what parents should do. Sometimes it is wise to answer a what-would-you-do question with a pleasant remark which can lead into a discussion of the experience of others in similar situations. This gives the parent several alternative ideas that can be tried rather than one direct answer. In reality, the teacher cannot always tell what will work for that parent, but the teacher can safely share what has been tried at school and what has worked and what has not worked in other instances.

Information is quite often given in conferences that deals with some very personal desires and feelings of the parents, or with some of their personal difficulties. Whatever is said should be held in strictest confidence by the teacher. The teacher must use good judgment in determining whether to divulge the information to others, such as the principal or guidance worker. In some cases, the child would be better served by withholding information given in confidence.

Many things are said in conferences which may surprise or even shock the teacher and severely test her ability not to pass judgment on the child or the family. The teacher who does much interviewing soon learns that a startled, shocked, surprised or disapproving action abruptly shuts off what is being said and may prevent open discussion of other important topics. The teacher's ability to be a good listener is essential. She can learn many things about the child that otherwise she would have no way of knowing.

Arguments with parents should be avoided. Most parents want to keep the interview friendly, but occasionally a parent who disagrees with a teacher's methods will make an accusing statement or question the teacher's competency. The teacher is fortunate if she can let these remarks roll off without bristling and go ahead with other points in the discussion. She may later be able to return to the issue in a different way in order to emphasize that she is trying to help the child.

Parents welcome being made to feel they are doing a good job with their youngster. No doubt they have discussed their child's immediate problems with the child until they are almost in despair about the success of their efforts. They wonder if Jill will ever learn to wash her hands before eating and if Henry will ever learn to hang up his coat. Yet the teacher says that Henry is helping to put toys away at school and that he no longer has to be reminded to hang up his coat. There are many positive things which can be said about most children, and the parent interview is a good time to say some of these. It will make for a much better conference, as well as a much better relationship with the parents, if they leave feeling that the teacher likes the child and does not spend all her time criticizing him.

Parents will feel they have had a better interview if they have an opportunity to talk about all the things that are on their minds. They usually have many questions, many observations of the child's behavior that they want to check with the teacher. Not all of what the parent wants to say will seem important to the teacher, but much will be said which provides additional insight into the family.

COMMUNITY RESOURCES

Because most early childhood programs have not been associated with public schools, they have not always considered themselves very much a part of the community. Sometimes participation in school activities has drawn the parents and staff into participation in activities of a sponsoring organization. Sometimes the program is community sponsored, in the sense that funds are provided by the community.

How to become a more integral part of community activity is a concern of quite a few educational programs. Some programs have found that to be recognized by the community they must reach out to it. Parents have made files of community resources that might become a part of the school program. Local industries, businesses, and places of interest have been visited by parents and teachers to find out if they are suitable places for the children to visit. Story hours have been arranged by the library; trips have been made to the local zoo, shoe repair shop, bakery, post office and lumber yard. Children have seen the occupations in which their parents and their neighbors are engaged. They have had local artisans come to the school to work and they have seen them in their own shops. In this way the school has become a very vital part of community life. Many community people do not understand early childhood education very well, but they like what they see and they recommend it to others in the community. Such a community is well on its way to being a contributor to the education of its younger children.

QUESTIONS FOR DISCUSSION

1. Work out a set of guidelines for the parent involvement program of a day care center.

2. Interview five parents and record the feelings they express about their children who are enrolled in nursery school. If you were the teacher, indicate how you would plan to talk with each of these parents about their children.

3. Talk to a parent in a cooperative nursery school, in Head Start, in a private nursery school. How do these parents feel about

their involvement in the school? How do you account for the differences?

4. Outline a series of group discussions for a small group of nursery school parents. Why did you select the particular topics you did?

5. Assume you are a new kindergarten teacher in a public school that has little or no contact with parents. What would you do to initiate additional contacts with parents? What kind of support would you need from the school administration to do this?

Selected References

CHAPTER 1 A POINT OF VIEW ABOUT EARLY CHILDHOOD EDUCATION

Anderson, Robert H., and Shane, Harold G. *As the Twig is Bent.* Boston: Houghton Mifflin, 1971. (Chapters 21–28—Curriculum: Theory, Practice and Evaluation.)

Battelle Memorial Institute. *Final Report on Preschool Education to Ohio Department of Education.* Columbus, Ohio: Battelle Memorial Institute, 1969. (Review of preschool research and recommendations for programs.)

Berson, Minnie Perrin. "Early Childhood Education," *American Education* 4 (1968):7–13.

Biber, Barbara. "A Learning-Teaching Paradigm Integrating Intellectual and Affective Processes." In *Behavioral Science Frontiern in Education,* edited by Eli M. Bower and William G. Hollister. New York: John Wiley and Sons, 1969.

Bloom, Benjamin S. *Stability and Change in Human Characteristics.* New York: Wiley, 1964.

Butler, Annie L. "Areas of Recent Research in Early Childhood Education," *Childhood Education* 48 (1971):143–147.

———. *Current Research in Early Childhood Education: A Compilation and Analysis for Program Planners.* Washington, D.C.: American Association of Elementary-Kindergarten-Nursery Educators, 1970.

Dennis, Wayne, and Najarian, Pergrouhi. "Development Under Environmental Handicap." In *Readings in Child Psychology,* 2nd ed., edited by Wayne Dennis. Englewood Cliffs, N.J.: Prentice-Hall, 1963, pp. 315–331.

Directions Seminar. *The Children We Neglect: A Call for Action.* Washington, D.C.: National Committee for Children and Youth, 1971.

Education Commission of the States Task Force on Early Childhood Education. *Early Childhood Development: Alternatives for Program Im-*

plementation in the States. Denver: Education Commission of the States, 1971.

Evans, Ellis D. *Contemporary Influences in Early Childhood Education.* New York: Holt, Rinehart and Winston, 1971.

Federal Panel on Early Childhood. *Federal Interagency Day Care Requirements,* Pursuant to Sec. 522(d) of the Economic Opportunity Act, ERIC No. ED 126 145. Washington, D.C.: Government Printing Office, 1968.

Frost, Joe L. *Early Childhood Rediscovered.* New York: Holt, Rinehart and Winston, 1968. (Book of readings relative to early childhood programs.)

———, and Payne, Billy L. "Hunger in America: Scope and Consequences." In *Nutrition and Intellectual Growth in Children.* Washington, D.C.: Association for Childhood Education International, 1969.

Gordon, Ira J. "The Beginnings of the Self: The Problem of the Nurturing Environment," *Phi Delta Kappan* 50 (1959):375–378.

Grotberg, Edith H. *Review of Research, 1965 to 1969.* ERIC No. ED 028 308. Washington, D.C.: Project Head Start, Office of Economic Opportunity, 1969.

Heath, Douglas. "The Education of Young Children at the Crossroads," *Young Children* 25 (1969):73–84.

Heffernan, Helen. "Early Childhood Education: Influence on the Elementary School," *Today's Education* 59 (1970):41–42.

Hess, Robert D., and Croft, Doreen J. *Teachers of Young Children.* Boston: Houghton Mifflin, 1972. (Chapter 1—Early Education as a Career.)

Hunt, Joseph McVicker. *The Challenge of Incompetence and Poverty.* Urbana: University of Illinois Press, 1969.

———. "Has Compensatory Education Failed? Has It Been Attempted?" *Harvard Educational Review* 39 (1969):278–300.

———. *Intelligence and Experience.* New York: Ronald Press, 1961.

Jensen, Arthur R. "How Much Can We Boost I Q and Scholastic Achievement?" *Harvard Educational Review* 39 (1969):1–123.

Keyserling, Mary D. "Day Care: Crisis and Challenge," *Childhood Education* 48 (1971):59–67.

Krech, Davod. "Psychoneurobiochemeducation," *Phi Delta Kappan* 50 (1969):370–375.

Lane, Mary B., et al. *Nurseries in Cross-Cultural Education, Final Report.* San Francisco State College, School of Education, PHS Grant No. R11 MHO 1976 and R01 MH 14782, 1971.

Margolin, Edythe. "Conservation of Self-Expression and Aesthetic Sensitivity in Young Children," *Young Children* 23 (1968):155–160.

Scrimshaw, Nevin S. "Infant Malnutrition and Adult Learning," *Saturday Review* 51 (1968):64–66.

Senn, Milton J. E. "Early Childhood Education: For What Goals?" *Children* 16 (1969):8–13.

Skeels, Harold. *Adult Status of Children with Contrasting Early Life Experiences.* Monograph of the Society for Research in Child Development, 32 (1966):1–68.

Starkweather, Elizabeth. *Potential Creative Ability and the Preschool Child.* ERIC No. ED 108 900. Stillwater: Oklahoma State University, 1966, 9 pp.

Torrance, E. Paul. *The Creative-Aesthetic Approach to School Readiness and Measured Creative Growth,* ERIC No. ED 017 344. Athens: University of Georgia, Research and Development Center in Educational Stimulation, 1967.

———. "Must Creative Development be Left to Chance?" in *Creativity: Its Educational Implications,* edited by John C. Gowan et al. New York: John Wiley and Sons, 1967.

———. "Toward the More Humane Education of Gifted Children." In *Creativity: Its Educational Implications,* edited by John C. Gowan, George D. Damos, and E. Paul Torrance. New York: John Wiley and Sons, 1967.

Universal Opportunity for Early Childhood Education. Washington, D.C.: National Education Association, 1966.

Wann, Kenneth, et al. *Fostering Intellectual Development in Young Children.* New York: Bureau of Publications, Teachers College, 1962.

Weber, Evelyn. *Early Childhood Education: Perspectives on Change.* Worthington, Ohio: Charles A. Jones Publishing Co., 1970.

Westman, Jack C., et al. "Nursery School Behavior and Later School Adjustment," *American Journal of Orthopsychiatry* 37 (1967):725–731.

Zigler, Edward. *Training the Intellect Versus Development of the Child,* ERIC No. ED 034 573. New Haven, Conn.: Yale University, 1968.

CHAPTER 2 ORGANIZATIONAL AND ADMINISTRATIVE DIVERSITY IN EARLY CHILDHOOD PROGRAMS

Anderson, Robert H. "Schools for Young Children: Organizational and Administrative Considerations," *Phi Delta Kappan* 50 (1969):381–385.

"Business Starts to Fill Preschool Void," *Nation's Schools,* 84 (1969):24.

Child Welfare League of America. *Child Welfare League of America*

Standards for Day Care Service. New York: Child Welfare League of America, 1960.

Class, N. E. "Licensing for Child Care," *Children* 15 (1968):188–192.

Costin, L. B. "New Directions in the Licensing of Child Care Facilities," *Child Welfare,* 49 (1970):64–71.

"Day Care, Not Baby-Sitting," *Saturday Review* 52 (1969):75.

Education Commission of the States Task Force in Early Childhood Education. *Early Childhood Education: Alternatives for Program Implementation.* Denver: Education Commission of the States, 1971.

Evans, E. Belle, et al. *Day Care.* Boston: Beacon Press, 1971. (How to plan, develop, and operate a day care center.)

Green, Marjorie M., and Woods, Elizabeth L. *A Nursery School Handbook for Teachers and Parents.* Sierra Madre, Calif.: Sierra Madre Community Nursery School Association, 1963. (Cooperative nursery school handbook.)

Keliher, Alice V. "Parent and Child Centers: What They Are, Where They are Going," *Children* 16 (1969):63–66.

Keyserling, Mary D. "Day Care: Crisis and Challenge," *Childhood Education* 48 (1971):59–67.

Mann, M. J. "Laboratory Nursery School at the Liberal Arts College: Some Normative Data," *Young Children* 24 (1968):15–17.

Murphy, Lois B. "Multiple Factors in Learning in the Day Care Center," *Childhood Education* 45 (1969):311–320.

National Council of State Consultants in Elementary Education. *Education for Children Under Six.* Cheyenne, Wyo.: National Council of State Consultants in Elementary Education, 1968.

Office of Economic Opportunity. *Daily Program I.* Project Head Start Bulletin No. 4. Washington, D.C.: Office of Economic Opportunity, 1965.

———. *Medical.* Project Head Start Bulletin No. 2. Washington, D.C.: Office of Economic Opportunity, 1965.

———. *Nutrition.* Project Head Start Bulletin No. 3. Washington, D.C.: Office of Economic Opportunity, 1965

———. *Parents.* Project Head Start Bulletin No. 6. Washington, D.C.: Office of Economic Opportunity, 1965.

———. *The Staff.* Project Head Start Bulletin No. 1. Washington, D.C.: Office of Economic Opportunity, 1965.

———. *Volunteers.* Project Head Start Bulletin No. 5. Washington, D.C.: Office of Economic Opportunity, 1965.

Peet, Anne. "Why Not Enough Public School Kindergartens?" *Young Children* 21 (1965):112–116.

Riley, Clara M. C. *Head Start in Action.* West Nyack, N.J.: Parker Publishing Co., 1967.

Scarr, S. "Needed: A Complete Head Start," *Elementary School Journal* 69 (1969):236–241.

Steiert, K. "So You Want to Have a Public School Kindergarten," *Virginia Journal of Education* 61 (1968):18–20.

Taylor, Katherine W. *Parent Cooperative Nursery Schools, Parents and Children Learn Together.* New York: Teachers College Press, 1968.

Todd, Vivian Edmiston, and Heffernan, Helen. *The Years Before School.* New York: Macmillan, 1970. (See Chapter I, Preschool Education in America Today.)

CHAPTER 3 PROVIDING ADEQUATE STAFF

Abbott, J. M. "Men in Kindergarten," *Educational Digest* 33 (1968):45.

Association for Childhood Education International. *Preparation Standards for Teachers in Early Childhood Education.* Washington, D.C.: Association for Childhood Education International, 1967.

Bacmeister, Rhoda. *Teachers for Young Children: The Person and the Skills.* New York: Early Childhood Education Council of New York, n.d.

Berman, S. P. "Report on a CWLA Pilot Project to Train New Child Care Workers," *Child Welfare* 49 (1970):79–94.

Boguslawski, Dorothy Beers. *Guide for Establishing and Operating Day Care Centers for Young Children.* New York: Child Welfare League of America, 1966.

Brophy, Jere E. "Mothers as Teachers of Their Own Preschool Children: The Influence of Socioeconomic Status and Task Structure on Teaching Specificity," *Child Development* 41 (1970):79–94.

Child Welfare League of America. *Child Welfare League of America Standards for Day Care Service.* New York: Child Welfare League of America, 1960.

Couvillion, M. "Working with the Untrained Teacher," *Young Children* 24 (1968):37–41.

Durrett, M. E. "Attitudinal Outcomes of Eight-week Head Start Teacher-Training Programs with the Parental Attitude Research Instrument, *Childhood Education* 46 (1969):115–117.

Education Commission of the States Task Force on Early Childhood Education. *Alternatives for Program Implementation in the States.* Denver: Education Commission of the States, 1971.

Garrison, D. J. "Teacher Aide and Child Care Program," *Today's Education* 59 (1970):32.

Gross, Dorothy W. "Teachers of Young Children Need Basic Inner Qualities," *Young Children* 23 (1967):107–110.

Haberman, Martin, and Persky, Blanche, eds. *Preliminary Report of the Ad Hoc Joint Committee on the Preparation of Nursery and Kindergarten Teachers.* Washington, D.C.: National Commission on Teacher Education and Professional Standards, N.E.A., 1969.

Johnston, John M. "Of Hairy Arms and a Deep Baritone Voice, A Symposium: Men in Young Children's Lives," *Childhood Education* 47 (1970):144–147.

Katz, Lilian G. "Teaching in Preschools: Roles and Goals," *Children* 17 (1970):42–48.

MacDonald, S. "Home Economics Course Prepares Child Care Aides," *School and Community* 56 (1970):31.

Malnuccio, A. N. "Using a Step Toward Professionalism in Training of Child Care Staff," *Child Welfare* 49 (1970):165–167.

May, Charles R. "Men Teachers in Early Childhood Education: Which Direction Will They Take Now?" *Contemporary Education* 42 (1971):222–225.

Milgram, Joel I. "Sources of Manpower for the Preschool Classroom," *Childhood Education* 49 (1972):187–189.

Moustakas, Clark. *The Authentic Teacher.* Cambridge, Mass.: Howard A. Doyle Publishing Co., 1966.

National Council of State Consultants in Elementary Education. *Education for Children Under Six.* Cheyenne, Wyo.: NCSCEE, 1968. (Chapters 5 and 6—personnel needs and preparation.)

"No Girls (or Lady Teachers) Please," *Nation's Schools* 83 (1969):68–69.

"Preparation Standards for Teachers in Early Childhood Education—Nursery, Kindergarten, Primary," *Young Children* 23 (1967):79–80.

Schmitthauser, C. M. "Professionalization of Teaching in Early Childhood Education," *Journal of Teacher Education* 30 (1969):188–190.

Sell, Evelyn, "Is Nursery School Student Teaching Preparation for Elementary Student Teaching?" *Childhood Education* 43 (1967):516–519.

Stith, M., and Hoeflin, R. "Preschool Teacher Certification," *Journal of Home Economics* 59 (1967):371–373.

Zigler, Edward. *A New Child Care Profession: The Child Development Associate.* Paper presented at Annual Meeting of the National Association for the Education of Young Children, November 6, 1971, at Minneapolis, Minnesota.

CHAPTER 4 FACILITIES FOR EARLY CHILDHOOD PROGRAMS

Abramson, Paul. *Schools for Early Childhood.* New York: Educational Facilities Laboratories, 1970.

Baker, Katherine Read. "Extending the Indoors Outside." In *Housing for Early Childhood Education,* pp. 59–65. Washington, D.C.: Association for Childhood Education International, 1968.

"Bing Nursery School," *Childhood Education* 45 (1969):513–516.

Bureau of Child Development and Parent Education. *Equipment for Children in Kindergarten.* Albany: New York State Education Department, 1960.

Caudill, William. "What Works and What Fails in School Design," *Nation's Schools* 79 (1967):85–116.

Chase, William W., and Berson, Minnie P. "Planning Preschool Facilities," *American Education* 2 (1966):7–11.

Corbett, W. "Plain Tile and Otherwise," *National Elementary Principal* 47 (1969):55.

Dattner, Richard. *Design for Play.* New York: Van Nostrand Reinhold, 1969.

Gardner, Dwayne E. "An Ideal Environment for Learning." In *Housing for Early Childhood Education,* pp. 3–6. Washington, D.C.: Association for Childhood Education International, 1968.

Graves, Ben E. "Modernization," *Nation's Schools* 87 (1971):58–94.

Grey, A. "Creative Learning in Children's Playgrounds," *Childhood Education* 45 (1969):491–499.

Gross, D. W. "Equipping a Classroom for Young Children," *Young Children* 24 (1968):100–103.

Haase, Ronald W. *Designing the Child Development Center.* Washington, D.C.: Office of Child Development, 1969.

———. "How to Plan a Preprimary Classroom," *Nation's Schools* 77 (1966):50–54.

———. "Space Which Allows." In *Housing for Early Childhood Education.* Washington, D.C.: Association for Childhood Education International, 1968.

Howell, R. R. "Spring Comes to a City Nursery School Playground," *Young Children* 23 (1968):196–201.

"How Schools Can Find the Proper Playground Surface," *Nation's Schools* 79 (1967):78.

"It's Like a Cozy Suburban Home, But Edina's Kindergarteners Find It's Their School," *Nation's Schools* 83 (1969):120.

Jefferson, Ruth E. "Indoor Facilities." In *Housing for Early Childhood Education,* pp. 41–52. Washington, D.C.: Association for Childhood Education International, 1968.

Lande, Winifred D. "Climate Makes a Difference: In Alaska." In *Housing for Early Childhood Education,* pp. 27–28. Washington, D.C.: Association for Childhood Education International, 1968.

Lipson, R. "Mobile Preschool," *Young Children* 24 (1969):154–156.

Noecker, Albertine. "A Doll Corner Upstairs," *Young Children* 25 (1969): 102–103.

Osmon, Fred Linn. *Patterns for Designing Children's Centers.* New York: Educational Facilities Laboratories, 1971.

Pfluger, L. W., and Zola, J. M. "Room Planned by Children," *Young Children* 24 (1969):337–341.

Rosner, Sophie. "A Place in Space." In *Housing for Early Childhood Education,* pp. 67–70. Washington, D.C.: Association for Childhood Education International, 1968.

Stone, Jeannette G. *Play and Playgrounds.* Washington, D.C.: National Association for the Education of Young Children, 1970.

Zellner, Mary. "Climate Makes a Difference: In Florida." In *Housing for Early Childhood Education,* pp. 29–31. Washington, D.C.: Association for Childhood Education International, 1968.

CHAPTER 5 ADMISSION AND GROUPING POLICIES

A Comparison of Reading Readiness Achievement of Kindergarten Children of Disparate Entrance Ages. ERIC No. ED 033 745. New York: Queens College, City University of New York.

American Association of School Administrators. *Entrance Age Policies.* ERIC No. 031 813. Washington, D.C.: National Education Association, 1968.

Battelle Memorial Institute. *Final Report on Preschool Education to Ohio Department of Education.* Columbus, Ohio: Battelle Memorial Institute, 1969. (Statute regarding attendance.)

Berson, Minnie P. "All-Day Kindergarten," *Today's Education* 57 (1968): 27–29.

Brunner, Catherine. "Early Admission-School Admissions Project," *Education Digest* 30 (1964):22–25.

The Effects of Mothers' Presence and Previsits on Children's Emotional Reactions to Starting to Nursery School. ERIC No. ED 034 596. Syracuse, N.Y.: Syracuse University.

"For Boys/Girls Only; Separate Classes for Boys and Girls and a Male Teacher in Charge," *Grade Teacher* 87 (1970):143–147.

Gorton, H. B. "For Better Results: A Full-Day Kindergarten," *Education* 89 (1969):217–221.

Harding, A. C. "Early School Admissions: A Baltimore Best Seller," *Today's Education* 58 (1969):57–58.

Hobson, J. R. "High School Performance of Underage Pupils Initially Admitted to Kindergarten on the Basis of Physical and Psychological Examination," Educational and Psychological Measurement 23 (1963):159–170.

Lane, Mary B., et al. *Nurseries in Cross-Cultural Education*. San Francisco State College, 1971. (Describes innovative grouping experiment.)

Read, Katherine, *The Nursery School*. 5th ed. Philadelphia: W. B. Saunders Co., 1971. (Chapter 10—Helping Children Adjust to New Experiences.)

Spodek, Bernard. *Teaching in the Early Years*. Englewood Cliffs, N.J.: Prentice-Hall, 1972. (Chapter 11—Organizing for Instruction.)

Todd, Vivian E., and Heffernan, Helen. *The Years Before School*. 2nd ed. New York: Macmillan, 1970. (Chapter 5—A Preschool Group.)

Weisdorf, Pearl. "A Comparison of 2,3,5 Days of Nursery School," *Young Children* 16 (1964):24–28.

Weiss, Rosalia. "The Validity of Early Entrance into Kindergarten," *The Journal of Educational Research* 56 (1962):53–54.

CHAPTER 6 HEALTH AND SAFETY POLICIES

Dayton, D. H. "Early Malnutrition and Human Development," *Children* 16 (1969):210–217.

Hartman, Evelyn E., and Olson, Al. "Health Program for Minneapolis Project Head Start 1966," *The Journal of School Health* 37 (1967):232–236.

Headley, Neith E. *Foster and Headley's Education in the Kindergarten*, 4th ed. New York: American Book Company, 1966. (See Chapter 6—Provisions for Physical Welfare.)

Hess, Robert D., and Croft, Doreen J. *Teachers of Young Children*. Boston: Houghton Mifflin, 1972.

Host, Malcolm S., and Heller, Pearl B. *Day Care Administration*. Child Development Series on Day Care, No. 7. Washington, D.C.: Office of Child Development, 1971.

Leeper, Sarah H., et al. *Good Schools for Young Children*. New York: Macmillan, 1968. (Chapter 15—Health and Safety.)

North, A. Frederick. *Day Care Health Services.* Child Development Series on Day Care, No. 6. Washington, D.C.: Office of Child Development, 1971.

Read, M. S. "Malnutrition and Learning," *American Education* 5 (1969): 11–14.

Sauer, Louis W. "Your Child's Health: Concerning Day Care," *The PTA Magazine* 62 (1967) :29–30.

Stone, Donald B., and Kudla, Kenneth J. "An Analysis of Health Needs and Problems as Revealed by A Selected Sample of Project Head Start Children," *The Journal of School Health* 37 (1967):470–476.

Todd, Vivian Edmiston, and Heffernan, Helen. *The Years Before School.* 2nd ed. New York: Macmillan, 1970.

Weintaub, David H. "The Preschool Child: Health Concepts." In *Early Childhood Education,* edited by Ira J. Gordon, chap. V. Seventy-first Yearbook of the National Society for the Study of Education. Chicago: University of Chicago Press, 1972.

CHAPTER 7 MANAGING SCHOOL FINANCES

Boguslawski, Dorothy B. *Guide for Establishing and Operating Day Care Centers for Young Children.* New York: Child Welfare League of America, 1968.

Education Commission of the States Task Force on Early Childhood Education. *Alternatives for Program Implementation in the States.* Denver: Education Commission of the States, 1971. (Appendix C—State Funding for Early Childhood Education.)

Evans, E. Belle, et al. *Day Care.* Boston: Beacon Press, 1971. (See Chapter 15, Planning a Budget, and Chapter 16, Raising Funds.)

Greenberg, P. "Low-Cost State Strategies with a New Look," *Compact* 3 (1969):26–31.

Host, Malcolm S., and Heller, Pearl B. *Day Care Administration.* Child Development Series, No. 7. Washington, D.C.: Office of Child Development, 1971.

Mushkin, S. "Cost of a Total Preschool Program in 1975," *Compact* 3 (1969):47.

National Council of State Consultants in Elementary Education. *Education for Children Under Six.* Cheyenne, Wyo.: National Council of State Consultants in Elementary Education, 1968.

Peterson, E. "Labor and Education," *Childhood Education* 46 (1969): 22–23.

CHAPTER 8 RECORDS AND REPORTS

Almy, Millie. *Ways of Studying Children*. New York: Bureau of Publications, Teachers College, Columbia University, 1959. (A manual for teachers.)

Butler, Annie L. *An Evaluation Scale for Four- and Five-Year-Old Children*. Bloomington, Ind.: Bulletin of the School of Education, Indiana University, 1965.

Christianson, Helen, et al. *The Nursery School*. Boston: Houghton Mifflin, 1961. (Chapter 4—Techniques of Observation and Record Keeping.)

Dowley, Edith M. "Cues for Observing Children's Behavior," *Childhood Education* 45 (1969):517–521.

Evans, E. Belle, et al. *Day Care*. Boston: Beacon Press, 1971. (See Appendix for example of form.)

Headley, Neith E. *Foster and Headley's Education in the Kindergarten*. 4th ed. New York: American Book Company, 1966. (See Chapter 23—Kindergarten Records and Reports.)

Leeper, Sarah H., et al. *Good Schools for Young Children*. New York: Macmillan, 1968. (Chapter 19—Recording the Development of Children.)

Read, Katherine. *The Nursery School*. 5th ed. Philadelphia: W. B. Saunders, 1971. Chapter 9—Making Observations.)

CHAPTER 9 PARENT AND COMMUNITY INVOLVEMENT IN SCHOOLS

Associaton for Childhood Education International. *Parents-Children-Teachers: Communication*. Washington, D.C.: The Association, 1969.

Auerbach, Aline B., and Roche, Sandra. *Creating a Preschool Center: Parent Development in an Integrated Neighborhood Project*. New York: John Wiley and Sons, 1971.

Ballard, Virginia and Strong, Ruth. *Parent-Teacher Conferences*. New York: McGraw-Hill, 1964.

Biber, Barbara. *What Do Children Need Most: From Parent, from Teacher?* New York: Bank Street College of Education Publications, 1967.

Brady, E. H. "Use of Videotapes in Parent Conferences," *Young Children* 23 (1968):276–280.

Bromberg, S. L. "Beginning Teacher Works With Parents," *Young Children* 24 (1968):75–80.

Chilman, Catherine S. "Some Angles on Parent-Teacher Learning," *Childhood Education* 48 (1971):119–125.

Conant, Margaret M., "Teachers and Parents: Changing Roles and Goals," *Childhood Education* 48 (1971):114–118.

Cutler, Marilyn H. "How Schools Prepare Parent Guidebooks," *Nation's Schools* 79 (1967):119–122.

Dady, Milan B. "Improving School-Community Relations," *Journal of Research and Development in Education* 5 (1972):91–94.

Evaluation Report: *Early Childhood Education Program, 1969 Field Test.* ERIC No. ED 041 626. Charleston, W. Va.: Appalachia Educational Laboratory, 1970, 204 pp.

Gray, Susan W., and Klaus, R. A. "The Early Training Project: A Seventh Year Report," *Child Development* 41 (1970):909–924.

Gordon, Ira. *Early Stimulation Through Parent Education: Final Report.* ERIC No. ED 033 912. Gainesville: University of Florida, 1969, 233 pp.

Gotkin, L. G. "Telephone Call: The Direct Line from Teacher to Family," *Young Children* 24 (1968):70–74.

Grissom, Catherine E. "Listening Beyond Words: Learning from Parents in Conferences," *Childhood Education* 48 (1971):138–140.

Grotberg, Edith H. "Role of the Parent in Fostering Early Learning," *Education* 89 (1968):35–39.

Handler, E. "Teacher-Parent Relations in Preschool," *Urban Education* 6 (1971):215–232.

Hayman, H. J. "Snap Judgment: A Roadblock to Progress on Parent Involvement," *Young Children* 23 (1968):291–293.

Hymes, James L. *Effective Home-School Relations.* Englewood Cliffs, N.J.: Prentice-Hall, 1956. (Not recent, but still one of the best references on understanding how teachers and parents may feel about each other.)

Jones, Elizabeth. "Involving Parents in Children's Learning," *Childhood Education* 47 (1970):126–130.

The Juniper Gardens Parent Cooperative Nursery: Final Progress Report. ERIC No. ED 032 920. Kansas City, Mo., 1968, 38 pp.

Karnes, Merle B., et al. *An Approach for Working with Mothers of Disadvantaged Children: A Pilot Project.* ERIC No. ED 017 335. Urbana: University of Illinois, n.d., 30 pp.

King, E. W. "Coffee Hour for Kindergarten Parents," *Instructor* 78 (1969): 110.

Langdon, Grace, and Stout, Irving W. *Teacher-Parent Interviews.* Englewood Cliffs, N.J.: Prentice-Hall, 1954.

Larrabee, M. M. "Involving Parents in Their Children's Day Care Experiences," *Children* 16 (1969):149–154.

Levenstein, Phyllis, "Learning Through (and from) Mothers," *Childhood Education* 48 (1971):130–134.

Miller, W. H. "When Mothers Teach Their Children," *Elementary School Journal* 70 (1969):38–42.

Moore, H. E., and Stout, I. W. *A Plan of Action for Parent-Child Educational Centers.* ERIC No. ED 027 959. Tempe: Arizona State University, 1968, 30 pp.

Nimnicht, Glenn. *A Progress Report on the Parent-Child Course and Toy Library.* ERIC No. ED 045 206. Berkeley, Calif.: Far West Laboratory for Educational Research and Development, 1970, 34 pp.

North, G. E., and Buchanan, O. L. "Maternal Attitudes in a Poverty Area," *Journal of Negro Education* 37 (1968):418–425.

Office of Economic Opportunity. *Parent Involvement.* Washington, D.C.: Office of Economic Opportunity, 1969.

Phelps, D. W. "Parent Perceptions of Cooperative Nursery School Evening Meetings: Implications for Professional Education," *Adult Leadership* 14 (1965):87–88.

Schaefer, Earl S. "Learning from Each Other," *Childhood Education* 48 (1971):2–7.

Weikart, David P. "Learning Through Parents: Lessons for Teachers," *Childhood Education* 48 (1971):135–137.

———, and Lambie, Dolores Z. "Preschool Intervention Through a Home Teaching Program." in *Disadvantaged Child,* edited by Jerome Helmuth, vol. 2, pp. 435–500. New York: Brunner Mazel, 1968.

Willman, B. "Parent Participation as a Factor in the Effectiveness of Head Start Programs," *Journal of Educational Research* 62 (1969):406–410.

Appendix A
Equipment and Supply Checklist

This equipment list is presented primarily as a guide for those who are organizing a new early childhood program or those who are seeking to supplement the supplies and equipment currently available to them. No distinction is made regarding the ages of the children in a program, although not all materials listed here would be necessary for the youngest children. Nor is any distinction made for the type of program. For example, cots are included on the list although they would not be needed in a program where children do not take a nap. Quantities of materials are estimated for twenty children, but they will vary according to the emphasis in a program. For example, a program that emphasizes art and creative activities will need more supplies in this area. If a great deal of time is to be spent outside, the amount and variety of outdoor equipment will vary.

Commercially prepared kits are not listed. These must be carefully evaluated in relation to each program and each staff. Prices for such kits are usually quite high, and the money might better be spent for basic equipment which would be more versatile, particularly for the youngest children.

Prices for equipment vary somewhat from company to company and therefore should be compared. Checking prices in the local area is highly recommended, as shipping costs can greatly add to the expense of the equipment. Some schools have found it desirable for the director and other members of the staff to go directly to a company and bring the supplies back when major amounts are purchased. Construction of items such as shelving, tables, and outdoor equipment may be done locally and can result in excellent equipment at a substantial saving of money.

INTEREST AREAS FOR THE CLASSROOM

Art

Brushes: 12 round, 1¼" in hair length, 9" handle
24 flat, ¾" to 1¼" spread

assorted smaller brushes to allow children to achieve varying effects

Chalk: large 1" in diameter, assorted colors and white
regular size, assorted colors and white

Charcoal: pencils or pieces

Clay: 200 pounds potters clay, dry or mixed
covered stone jar with wooden cover for keeping clay moist
12 clay boards, 12" x 12", or cover for table
25 pounds flour and 10 pounds salt with salad oil to make play dough
rolling pins or 2" doweling for rolling
various shaped cutters and tongue depressors to use with clay

Crayons: 10 dozen large pressed crayons, assorted colors

Easels: 2 double or wall easels

Erasers: art gum
felt for chalkboard

Felt-tip markers: 24, assorted colors, watercolor rather than ink

Felt or flannel board: 18" x 24"

Felt pieces: 12 9" x 12", assorted colors

Paint: 48 pints liquid tempera or 24 pounds powdered tempera or some of both
6 jars of red, yellow, blue, white
4 jars of black, green, brown, orange, turquoise, magenta
fingerpaint; 1 pint each yellow, red, green, blue, brown, black, or liquid starch and soap flakes for making fingerpaint
plastic jars with covers
watercolors, 10 sets semipermeable

Paraffin

Paper: gummed back, 8" x 10", assorted colors
manila; 3 reams, 18" x 24"
newsprint or inexpensive easel paper; 5 reams, 18" x 24"
fingerpaint paper; 3 reams, 18" x 24"
colored construction: 16 packages, assorted colors, 12" x 18", and 2 packages, assorted colors, 18" x 24"
tissue paper; 2 packages, 20" x 30", assorted colors
crepe paper, 20" x 7½', assorted colors
brown wrapping paper, 30" roll with holder

Paper bags: 100 8" x 14"

Paper cutter

Paste and glue: 1 gallon paste purchased in quarts
2 gallons liquid glue
jars or glue dispensers
sticks or brushes

Pencils
Plasticine: 5 pounds, single color
Pipe cleaners
Printing objects: corks, spools, sponges, string
Ruler: 6 twelve-inch, with ½" markings
Scissors: adult shears, 10"
20 with blunt points
String: carpet warp, colored
Tagboard: 25 sheets, 18" x 24", white
Tape: transparent, ½"
masking, ½"
mending, ¾"
adhesive, 1 roll, ½"
Tapestry needles: 3 packages, large size
Thread: black and white
Yarn: 1 skein each red, green, and yellow

Woodworking

Bits: ¼", ½", ¾", and 1"
Brace: adult size, 1½ pounds
Clamps: 3 C, 4" to 6" opening, metal
Coping saw: wooden handles, assorted blades
Hammers: 3 flat-headed claw, 10–15 ounces
Hand drill and drill sets
Nails: 2 pounds each 3d, 6d, 7d, and roofing nails
Nuts and bolts: assorted sizes
Sandpaper: 10 assorted, 000 to 3
Saws: 2 cross-cut, 12" and 16"
Screwdriver: 8" and 10"
Screws: assorted sizes
Square
Wall rack or cart for tools
Workbench: 20" x 48" x 24" high or sawhorses 8" x 30" x 24" high
Wood: scrap pieces of soft wood of various sizes and shapes
short lengths of wood dowels, spools
bottle tops or button molds for wheels

Housekeeping

Bed: wooden, 28" x 14" x 10" high, sturdy enough to hold a child
Brooms: 2 36" long

Carpet sweeper
Clothes bar: 30" x 36" high
Clothesline and pins
Clock, wooden with movable hands
Cooking utensils, aluminum, sturdy
Cupboard: wooden 12" x 20" x 40" high
Cutlery: aluminum or plastic
Dishes: tea set, unbreakable plastic or aluminum
Doll carriage: sturdy enough to hold a child
Dolls: 4 unbreakable, washable, easy to dress, including black dolls
Doll clothes: made to fit the dolls
Doll blankets
Dress-up clothes with chest
Dust mop
Dustpan and small counter brush
Empty food boxes
Iron and ironing board
Milk carrier and bottles
Mirror: full length
Mop: sponge, to mop up spills
Refrigerator: wooden, 12" x 20" x 36" high
Rocking chair: 10" to 12" seat height
Scales
Sink: wooden, with 2 plastic pans, 12" x 24" x 24" high
Stove: wooden, 12" x 20" x 24" high
Table and two chairs: table about 20" high, chair 12" high
Telephone: 2 wooden or plastic, with operating dial

Mathematics

Abacus
Calendar
Cash register
Clock
Counting blocks or rods
Counting frame
Dominoes: large
Flannel board: magnetic
Flannel-board figures: boxes of shapes, numerals, sets of objects
Match mates
Measures: plastic cups, pints, quarts, gallons
Number board showing 100

Number line
Numerals: large plastic or foam, easily handled
Pegboards
Ruler
Scales
Tape measure
Thermometer: large, easily readable
Toy money: paper and coins
Yardstick

Music

Instruments:
- autoharp: 12 bar
- drums: 2, with skin heads
- clappers: 3 or 4
- cymbals: 1 set
- melody bells or tone blocks: 1 set
- triangles: 3 or 4
- tambourines: 2 or 3
- sticks: enough for all the children
- jingle bells: enough for all the children
- xylophone: wooden

Phonograph: 2 if possible, 1 for teacher use and 1 for child use
Listening post: 4 to 6 earphones and jacks
Music books for use with young children
Piano and bench
Records: a wide variety including singing, listening, rhythms
Record caddy

Science

Animal cages: 36" x 36" x 36" for larger animals
12" x 38" x 14" tall with exercise wheel, all metal
Aquaria: for fish with pump and filter, for turtles
Bird cage: hanging
Cocoons: butterfly, moth
Compass: magnetic
Egg beaters: 3 rotary
Electrical invention kit: batteries, bells, switches, wires, etc.
Flower boxes and pots

Food for pets
Gardening tools: sturdy, junior size
Globe: 9" in diameter or larger
Hot plate
Incubator
Insect cage
Jars: glass bottles for specimens
Magnets: horseshoe or bar
Magnifying glass: at least 2½" in diameter
Mixing bowls: different sizes for use in cooking, 3 medium size for whipping soap and mixing dough
Pans: saucepan, baking sheet, cake pan
Plants
Plastic bags: assorted sizes
Pulleys
Prisms
Seeds and bulbs
Siphon tubes
Straws
Terrarium: 10" x 18" x 12" high
Tin cans: smooth opening, various sizes
Tablespoons, teaspoons, table knives
Tuning fork
Vases: assorted sizes
Watering can: plastic, long spout

Blocks

Block attachments: steering wheels, etc.
Boards: 8 6" x 3'
Building blocks: about 500 blocks including straight cut as well as circular and arched blocks
Hollow blocks: 36 12" x 12" x 6", with hand holes
12 24" x 12" x 6"
12 half units and triangles
Toys for use with blocks: 2 sets animals, wooden or soft plastic
farmyard set
airplanes, wooden
boats
cars, wooden
fire engines
play people

trains, wooden
trucks, wooden

Perceptual Motor Games and Activities

Lego blocks: 1 school set
Letters: large wooden or plastic
Lotto games
Mechanical form boards and simple bolt and lock sets
Pegboards and pegs: 4 boards with different colored pegs
Picture dominoes
Plastic shapes
Plastic squares or other plastic construction toys
Puzzles: 24 simple wooden jigsaw, 5–12 pieces, including frame for storage
Simple counting or matching games
Snap-n-play blocks

BASIC CLASSROOM FURNITURE AND SUPPLIES

Furniture

Bulletin boards
Chairs: at least 2 adult size
4 wicker, padded, or modern for the library unit, 12" seat height
20–25 wooden or plastic with metal tubing and silencers
Cabinets: with individual compartments containing storage space for individual children
Clock: electric wall clock
Cots: 20 52" long by 27" wide by 12" high
Desk: adult size with file drawers or file case
Drinking fountain: slant stream, 27" basin height
Sand table: with cover, 3' x 6' metal box 7" deep
Resting mats: 20" x 48", with durable plastic cover
Rug, if room is not partially carpeted, washable
Tables: 4–6, 20" to 22" high, of various sizes, plastic tops
1 library table, 36" in diameter, plastic top
Tool storage unit
Cabinets: should be built in sections light enough to be moved around
6–8 cabinets with open shelves for equipment frequently used by children

4 cabinets for storing equipment, cleaning supplies, toys not in use, etc.

Wastebaskets

Supplies

Broom: lightweight, adult size, long handled, push-broom style
Brush: counter style
Brushes, scrub: 2
Cleanser
Dust cloths
Dustpan, rubber tipped
Fire extinguisher
First-aid kit
Flag
Mop: small, lightweight, sponge
Paper towels and container
Pencil sharpener
Paper clips
Pins, safety
Soap dispenser
Sponges
Tissues
Toilet paper
Tongue depressors

AUDIO-VISUAL EQUIPMENT

For Each Classroom

Books for children: 25 to 30 in classroom at one time, with access to an unlimited supply, both story and reference
Bookcase or display rack
Pictures: carefully mounted and current
Puppets
Puppet stage
Maps: state and United States maps

Accessible to the Classroom

Filmstrip and slide collection with projector
Individual viewers for filmstrips and slides

Projector stand: 36" tall with swivel casters, rubber tires
Screen: portable, stand type
16-mm film collection with projector
Tape recorder

OUTDOOR EQUIPMENT

Balls: 4, assorted sizes
Bean bags: can be made
Barrels: with both ends cut, screwed or nailed on platform to climb through
Bridges: nesting
Cars, trains, airplanes, trucks: large enough to ride on
Climbing rope: 8' over soft surface
Climbing tower (Each playground should contain several kinds of climbing apparatus, sometimes called a jungle gym, horizontal ladder, or other trade name. A locally constructed tree house might serve this purpose well.)
Crates: large wooden
Irish mail
Ladder: wooden, 4' x 14", light but sturdy
Planks: with cleats on end for walking boards or teeter totters, 8' x 8"
Punching bag: stuffed pillow or jeans hung within child's reach
Skipping ropes: solid wooden handles
Rocking boat: might be a wooden trough that can be attached to climber when a slide is desired
Sand box: with cover, large enough to hold several children
Sand toys: spades, pails, large spoons, sifters, small dishes, small cars, etc.
Swings: rope, canvas, or air cushion, preferably attached to a tree
Storage shed
Teeter-totter: 9' plank with 18" sawhorse
Tricycles: 16" ball-bearing with bicycle spokes
20" ball-bearing with bicycle spokes
Tire casings: to roll around or for swings
Wagon: rubber tires, 16" x 34" x 3½" deep
Water table: 22" x 48" x 6" deep
Water equipment: brushes, buckets, floating objects, funnels, sprinkling can, hose
Wheel barrow

Appendix B
Sample Forms for Records

A single set of forms for use in early childhood programs probably would not be adequate for all schools because of the variety of types of programs. Since the child spends a much greater amount of time in day care, it is necessary for a day care center to obtain extensive information about the child and the home. On the other hand, a nursery school which children attend two hours per day would not need as much information about such things as eating and sleeping habits since the school would not be guiding a child in these activities on an extensive basis.

The records included in this section are samples of the kind of information that might be obtained at the beginning of a school year. Some schools might prefer to obtain some of the information by personal interview instead of having the parent write it all out.

The records used should be unique to each school and each program. Often there are certain aspects of the population that need to be brought out or there are teachers who feel they need some kind of information that not all schools or teachers may want. Schools should feel free to develop their own records and should seek the reactions of parents, who often do not think schools need all the information requested.

APPLICATION FOR ____________ SCHOOL Date: ____________

Child's name ____
last first middle

Sex ____________________ Date of birth ________________________

Parent's name ____

Telephone number ____

Date when admission is desired ________________________________

Comments ____

____

____

OPEN FAMILY INFORMATION CARD

Child's name ____
last first middle name child is called

Home address ______________________ phone number __________

Father's name ____

Work address ______________________ phone number __________

Mother's name ____

Work address ______________________ phone number __________

Names(s) of persons who may call for the child

1. ______________________ 2. ______________________

3. ______________________ 4. ______________________

Emergency contact ______________________ phone number __________

Child's doctor ______________________ phone number __________

Allergies ____

MEDICAL STATEMENT FOR ADMISSION

Child's name ______________________ Date of examination __________

I do hereby give my permission for the attending physician to give to the authorized representative of ______________________ School any medical information which would be helpful for the care of my child.

Parent's signature ______________________

Part I: History

(May be completed by parent or medical staff)

If the child had any of the following conditions, what year?

Measles (3-day)	__________	Mumps	__________
(red)	__________	Scarlet fever	__________
Chicken pox	__________	Poliomyelitis	__________
Whooping cough	__________	Diabetes	__________
Diphtheria	__________	Hernia	__________
Rheumatic fever	__________	Otitis media	__________
Epilepsy	__________	Convulsions	__________
Heart disease	__________	Mental retardation	__________
Pneumonia	__________		

Any physical handicaps ____

____

Allergies ____

____

Immunizations	*First date*	*Revaccination*
Diphtheria	________	________
Tetanus	________	________
Whooping cough	________	________
Measles	________	________
Poliomyelitis	________	________
Smallpox	________	________
Typhus	________	________
Influenza	________	________
Other	________	________

List in chronological order all surgical procedures performed on the child.

Date	*Type of surgery*	*Results*

Summary of admissions to hospital ________________________________

____

____

Is child currently under the care of a doctor? If so, for what reason?

____

____

Part II:

(To be completed by physician)

Results of examination of:

Scalp	________	Weight	________
Eyes and vision	________	Heart	________
Ears and hearing	________	Pulse	________
Nose	________	Abdomen	________
Teeth and mouth	________	Genitalia	________
Throat	________	Extremities	________
Neck	________	Reflexes	________
Lymph glands	________	Rectum	________
Spine	________	Skin	________
Lungs	________	Thorax	________
Height	________		

Please indicate any condition which might affect this child's performance at school or any condition the staff should be aware of: ________________

____

____

Recommendations ______________________________________

____

____

The above named child has been given a routine medical examination and has been found free of infectious or contagious diseases.

Signature of physician ____________________

INFORMATION FORM
SCHOOL

Child's name ____________________________ Date __________
last first middle

Name child is called ____________________ Birthdate __________

Address ________________________ Phone number __________

Other persons living in the household:

Name	*Relationship*	*Birthdate*

Type of dwelling: House ____ Duplex ____ Apartment ____ Rooms ____

Previous school experience ______________________________

____

Developmental History

Type of birth: Normal ______ Premature ______ Any complications ______

Age child began sitting ________ Crawling ________ Walking ________

Is child a good climber? __________ Does he fall easily? __________

Age child began talking __________ Current language abilities __________

Any difficulties in speaking? ________ Other languages spoken ________

Sleeping

What is child's bedtime? ________ What time does he get up? ________

Is he ready for sleep? ________ Does he have his own room? ________

His own bed? ________ Whom does he share with, if shared? ________

Does child have sleep disturbances? ________________________________

What is child's mood on awakening? ________________________________

Does child take naps? ________ From when ________ to ________

Does child tire easily? ________ Under what conditions? ________

Do you have any particular concerns about your child's sleeping habits? ________

Eating

Please describe the diet and pattern of eating of your child in the course of a day. ________________________________

Does the child enjoy eating? ________________________________

What are his favorite foods? ________________________________

What foods are refused? ________________________________

Does he feed himself? ____ With spoon? ____ With fork? ____ hands? ____

Do you have particular concerns about your child's eating habits? ________

Toilet Habits

Is your child toilet trained for urine? ________ For bowels? ________

If so, at approximately what age did he become trained? ________

What word is used for urination? ________ For bowel movement? ________

How frequently do accidents occur? ________________________________

How does the child react to them? ________________________________

Does he need help with toileting? ________________________________

Does the child wet the bed at night? ________ How often? ________

Do you have any particular concerns about your child's toilet habits? ________

Social and Emotional Behavior

Nervous habits: Does the child have temper tantrums? ________ Frequent upset stomachs? ________ Does he cry easily? ________ Does he suck his thumb or fingers? ________ Bite his nails? ________ Handle his body? ________ How would you describe his characteristic behavior? calm ________ excitable ________ easily upset ________ whining ________ happy ________ cheerful ________ negative ________ cooperative ________

With what age child does your child usually play? ____________________
____

Into how many homes does he go frequently? ____________________

How many playmates come to his house frequently? ____________________

What kind of group contacts does the child have? ____________________

How does he get along with his brothers and sisters? ____________________

Does he enjoy playing alone? ____________________

How does he relate to strangers? ____________________

How does he relate to friendly adults? ____________________

What makes him mad or upset? ____________________

How does he show these feelings? ____________________

What do you find is the best way to handle him? ____________________
____

What kind of discipline is usually used and by whom? ____________________
____

What are his favorite toys? ____________________
____

Is he frightened of any of the following? animals ______ rough children ______ loud noises ______ sirens ______ dark ______ storms ______ water ______

Describe his special interests. ____________________

Has he had any travel experiences? ____________________

Are there particular ways you think we might be able to help your child?
____
____

PARENT PARTICIPATION FORM

Name ________________________________ Date ____________

In order to include the parents in our programs and give them a share in their child's experiences, we are inviting you to take part in our program if you care to do so. This participation is voluntary. We will be glad if you can participate, but if you cannot, we will understand.

Please check any of the items below which you might like to do. Feel free to add others that we may have overlooked. We will work the activities in as they fit in with the children's interests and other planned experiences. We would also appreciate knowing times that are convenient for you.

______ I can help on excursions or trips.

______ I can help at parties and special occasions.

________ I can come regularly for part of a day to prepare materials and aid in activities. Please indicate any special day.

________ I can tell stories.

________ I can read to children or write the stories they dictate.

________ I can play a musical instrument. Name instrument.

________ We have collections such as pictures, shells, rocks which we would be glad to share with the children. Name collection.

________ I have special interests such as cooking, sewing, gardening which I would share with the children. Name.

________ I can help set up special activities such as a grocery store, post office, etc.

________ We have pets I would be glad to share with the school for a day.

________ I can help in the physical education area in assessing the development of individual skills.

________ List any other ways you would be willing to help.

____

____

____

____

____

Materials for our art scrap box, such as buttons, cloth, boxes, and wood scrap, are often needed. We also need new dress-up clothes for both girls and boys from time to time. You may send these by your child at any time during the year.

EXCURSION PERMISSION

I hereby give permission for my child or children to engage in school-sponsored excursions. I understand that these excursions may be taken either by bus, car, or on foot.

Signed ________________________

Date ________________________

Index